ST. MARY'S COL... LIBRARY
ST. MAR... C0-AJW-145

PIONEERS OF
AMERICAN ECONOMIC THOUGHT
IN THE NINETEENTH
CENTURY

PIONEERS OF AMERICAN ECONOMIC THOUGHT IN THE NINETEENTH CENTURY

BY

ERNEST TEILHAC

Professor of Political Economy,
Saint Joseph's University
Beirut, Syria

Authorized English
Translation

BY

E. A. J. JOHNSON

NEW YORK / RUSSELL & RUSSELL

FIRST PUBLISHED IN 1936
BY THE MACMILLAN COMPANY
REISSUED, 1967, BY RUSSELL & RUSSELL
A DIVISION OF ATHENEUM HOUSE, INC.
BY ARRANGEMENT WITH E. A. J. JOHNSON
L. C. CATALOG CARD NO: 66−27162

Reprinted from a copy in the collections of
The New York Public Library

PRINTED IN THE UNITED STATES OF AMERICA

27292

TRANSLATOR'S PREFACE

The multiple influences of English and French thought on the evolution of American political ideas are familiar to all students of American history and government. Quite properly, Americans believe that the combination of ideas achieved in the new world is not only unique, but politically and socially significant. About our indigenous economic thought, however, there has been no similar enthusiasm; indeed, not only have Americans been modest about this portion of their intellectual achievement, but for the most part essentially apologetic. It is within the realm of probability, however, that this undue modesty may be largely the consequence of a faulty understanding of the actual content of American economic thought. At any rate, few Americans have any comprehensive idea of the philosophical ingredients of their native brand of economics. Nor should they be harshly blamed. A far more complex interaction of English and French influences characterized American economic thought in the nineteenth century than is ordinarily realized. It really takes a foreigner, and especially a Frenchman, to pick out these intermeshed strands and to signalize just how the several strands were altered and modified by American economic conditions. It is precisely because M. Teilhac has so skillfully traced the complex interaction of French and English influences, and has indicated how the borrowings of American writers were modified under the force of American environment, that his monographs on Raymond, Carey, and

George are peculiarly significant. Moreover, they are not really monographs; a fundamental continuity underlies the changing current of economic ideas which not only gives unity to American economic thought, in spite of differences, but which indicates also the probable future trend of economic thought and ideology. Besides, M. Teilhac has done more than these immediate tasks. By interspersing comparative studies, he has indicated the similarities and the contrasts between American writers and a number of contemporary theorists. The benefits are obviously double: a clearer view of these similar or contrasting thinkers, together with a more ample appreciation of the American pioneers of economics.

A novice could scarcely have selected a more inconvenient book to translate; the style is involved, the subject matter complex. Fortunately, I have received generous criticism, and I therefore hope that my translation, although not felicitous, is reasonably faithful. If this be the reader's verdict, a large portion of the credit should go to my wife, who helped me unsparingly in preparing a first draft, to my gracious Oxford companion, William Crane, who undertook the wearisome task of verifying the first draft, and to B. L. Rideout, who checked the final draft for translation errors. Finally, I owe a very real debt to the genial and charming author of this book, M. Teilhac, not merely for his help in explaining more fully some of his interpretative devices, but for the gracious hospitality which he extended to Mrs. Johnson and myself at Poitiers.

E. A. J. J.

"THE CEDARS"
10 PARK TOWN
OXFORD.

AUTHOR'S PREFACE

The Double American Synthesis

Economic life in America is unusually large, not only in the very dimensions of its continental free trade or in the extent of its trust movement, but also in the rapidity of its evolution. The compression of time, involved in this evolution, has resulted in a magnification of the effect. As a consequence, American economic life is a vast panorama presented in such a perspective that everything is magnified; ten nations in one and ten centuries in one!

In thought, as well as in material achievement, has rapid evolution taken place. The nineteenth century in America was marked by a precipitous passage from mercantilism to physiocracy, from physiocracy to economic liberalism, from liberalism to protection and socialism. This intellectual metamorphosis, by and large, was a passage from the English to the French tradition, an abandonment of the French tradition for the Anglo-German, and finally, a return from the Anglo-German to the French tradition.

At the beginning of the nineteenth century, the United States, like France, lagged behind other countries in economic thought. In the twentieth century the United States and France tend again to converge in doctrinal advance. It was the naturalism of early American economic life which captivated the French writers of the eighteenth century while it is the rapid transition of America to a capitalistic economy which arouses French criticism today. Yet the individual naturalism which the United States originally embraced by reason of its physiocratic agrarianism is now being rediscovered in social rationalism.

For does not advanced social evolution, as represented in America by Henry George, really end by establishing a state of nature which is essentially the reflection of the Rousseauistic hypothesis which was fairly real in the America of Thomas Jefferson's time?

The purpose of this study is simply to sketch this living synthesis which presents a field of comparative economics, *par excellence.*

TABLE OF CONTENTS

PIONEERS OF AMERICAN ECONOMIC THOUGHT IN THE NINETEENTH CENTURY

CHAPTER I

THE ECONOMIC POLITICS OF DANIEL RAYMOND

SECTION I

The Predecessors of Raymond—From Benjamin Franklin to the Conflict between Hamilton and Jefferson

The history of nineteenth-century economic thought in the United States really begins with Benjamin Franklin, who, from 1706 to 1790, lived in the colonial milieu of Rip Van Winkle. Doubtless it was during his sojourns abroad that he came to recognize the true characteristics of his own country. He was shocked by the social misery which existed in England; in comparison, Franklin regarded every Indian as a gentleman! What a contrast between that commercial Albion, which was already becoming industrial, and America, basically agricultural! What a contrast between the cruel and unnatural artifice of an old society and the youthful liberty of the new world!

In France, the individualism which Franklin cherished was to find its means of expression in social rationalism, both political and economic. For whereas in France, political conditions were less advanced than in England,

1

economic conditions were also backward. Yet at the same time that a forward-going rationalism flourished in France, there survived, alongside of it, a deep-rooted individual naturalism. A most artificial political structure was built upon a fundamentally agrarian economic mass. In politics, therefore, one could more readily look forward to the recovery of a wholesome individual naturalism since economic conditions would tend to permit it.

Franklin went to France for the first time in 1767. The following year he received a collection of the works of Quesnay and Dupont. In 1769, appeared his most physiocratic work: *Positions to be Examined Concerning National Wealth*. Due to historical circumstances, he returned to France, in 1776. He prepared articles for the *Ephémérides du Citoyen* and he published his "Reflections on the Augmentation of Wages" in *Le Journal d'Économie Publique*. Not only was he closely associated with Quesnay and Dupont, but with Mirabeau and Turgot. He corresponded with Le Roy, Condorcet, La Rochefoucauld, Veillard, Morellet and Chaumont. He was presented to Voltaire. In brief, it was in France that Franklin found theoretical justification for the practical controversy between England and America. It was in France, also, at the awakening of American independence, that he found not only military assistance but legal sanction.

The naturalism of Franklin is essentially physiocratic; it rests upon American and French agrarianism. It is therefore incorrect to look upon him as the father of the labor theory of value. The ideas of Sir William Petty (with which he had become familiar, in 1724, in London) were quickly superseded by those of the Physiocrats. The value of any object, said Franklin, is determined by the labor necessary to provide a producer with subsistence. Agriculture is the chief way, the only honest way, to generate national wealth and to assure the well-being of a nation's population. In accordance with this theory, Franklin recommended early marriages since more people meant more producers and more wealth. But he did not follow the Physiocrats step by step. Like Turgot, he explained the phenomenon of interest by showing that capital could purchase land which would yield rent. Before the time of J. B. Say (who translated *Poor Richard's Almanac*, in 1794) he held that a skilled trade is as valuable as an estate of land. In a letter to Benjamin Vaughn, he distinguished productive from unproductive consumption. He dissociated the value of metal as bullion from its value as money. He pointed out that the cheapness of export commodities depends less upon the lowness of wages than upon other costs of production. Finally, in a series of object lessons, clothing most general ideas in concrete examples, he illustrated by anecdotes that goods exchange for goods.

With Franklin's modified naturalism, co-incided a vigorous rationalism. If one is sure that the principle is good, said he, one must put it into effect. Nevertheless, Franklin, the liberal, was as much opposed to social intervention in favor of the poor as to political intervention in favor of the rich. Although he favored direct taxation and absolute free trade, he advocated certain custom duties. He had hoped to negotiate commercial treaties with many nations but owing to the opposition of the Continental Congress, he had to content himself with treating with Prussia alone.

What was to be the future of this remarkable synthesis? After Franklin one can scarcely ignore Dickinson, whose *Letters to a Gentleman* contain correct ideas concerning trade and money. Neither can one overlook Pelatiah Webster who, in his *Political Essays on the Nature and Operations of Money* (published in Philadelphia, in 1791) revealed himself a vigorous opponent of a forced currency.

Meantime, beginning in 1794, a French emigré, Tanguy de la Boissière, edited in Philadelphia the first journal of political economy to be published in America: *Le Niveau de L'Europe et de L'Amérique Septentrionale.*

The most important names in early American economic discussion, however, were those of Hamilton and John Adams, on the one hand; Jefferson and John Taylor, on the other. The first group is represented by a tract, written in 1786: *A Defense of the Constitution of the Government of the United States Against the Attack of M. Turgot in His Letter to Dr. Price.* The other group is represented by the *Inquiry into the Principles and Policy of the Government of the United States,* which appeared in 1814, at Fredericksburg. One group represents reviving aristocratic monarchism, rising industrial capitalism, anglophile federalism (all of which were the aspirations of the North and later of the East). The other group represents a democratic spirit, physiocratic agrarianism, francophile republicanism (the aspirations of the South and later of the West). This cleavage between the two groups represents the destruction of the synthesis which Franklin had attempted. The duty, or the honor, as the case may be, of accomplishing this demolition was to be the lot of Hamilton.

The ideas of Alexander Hamilton (1757–1804) are a curious blend. They may be compared to the relation which exists between the classical doctrine of J. B. Say and physiocracy, and to the relation which exists between List's teachings and the classical doctrines. Hamilton's *Report on Public Credit* appeared in 1790. The following year, in his famous *Report on Manufactures,* he resumed and developed the ideas which he had enunciated earlier in *The Federalist.* These ideas arrange themselves around two centers: an industrial economy and protection. Labor, said Hamilton, is no more productive in agriculture than in industry;

land is only one form of capital. Goods exchange for goods, and the prosperity of agriculture depends upon the prosperity of industry. As opposed to the Physiocrats, Hamilton believed protection was necessary to develop industry and to insure an harmonious growth of American economic conditions. In order to prevent American industry from being smothered in the cradle by European competition, Hamilton advanced the still vigorous theory of international equalization of costs of production by means of import duties. Although Hamilton was merely opportunistically a bi-metalist, he advocated a central bank on principle. Hamilton's ideal, it should be clear, was a national economy which would insure political security and economic prosperity.

His influence, not only upon List, but upon Daniel Raymond and Henry C. Carey is patent. Yet the doctrinal characteristic of the nineteenth-century American economists after Hamilton was the recovery of the synthesis which Franklin had effected. In the writings of these later economists, the ideas of Jefferson and Taylor survived to such a degree that while the economic practice of the United States progressively approached that of England and whereas the facts continued more and more to support the reasoning of Hamilton, nevertheless American economic theory tended to react violently against the Hamiltonian tradition. Henry George illustrates this reaction. In short, one may say that the evolution of American economic thought in the nineteenth century consists, first, of a combination of the ideas which we designate as Jeffersonian and Hamiltonian, followed by a transition from Hamiltonian ideas to those purely Jeffersonian, a passage, indeed, from a sphere of facts to a reaction against facts.[1]

[1] Bourgeois, V. A., *Benjamin Franklin en France,* 1906; Chinard, G., *Jefferson et les Idéologues,* Paris, 1925; Faÿ, B., *L'Esprit Ré-*

SECTION II

Daniel Raymond's Originality

The economic works of Daniel Raymond reflect the contrast between American and European economic environment. They reveal the relativity of economic doctrines not only because they represent a reaction against the classical school but because the form of this reaction was different from the forms which would have been taken in the old world. Raymond's reaction against the classical doctrines crystallizes around three central ideas, three ideas whose development is unfinished today.[1]

SECTION III

A Critique of the Confusion of Private Interest with Public Interest

The chief criticism which Raymond levied against his predecessors was that they had confused the individual with the state, by presuming that whatsoever concerned the individual also concerned the state. From this hypothesis, said Raymond, arose a false conception of political economy.[2]

The mercantilist error of identifying money and national wealth and of confusing the interest of a particular

volutionnaire en France et aux États-Unis à la fin du XVIIIᵉ Siècle, Paris, 1925; Franklin, Benjamin, *Poor Richard's Almanac;* Hale, E. H., *Franklin in France,* Boston, 1887, *2 vols.;* Morse, J. T., *Benjamin Franklin,* Boston, 1889; Vandenberg, A. H., *The Greatest American, Alexander Hamilton,* New York, 1921; Wetzel, W. A., *Benjamin Franklin as an Economist* (Johns Hopkins University Studies 1895); Beard, C. A., *Economic Origins of Jeffersonian Democracy,* New York, 1915.

[1] Raymond, Daniel, *Thoughts on Political Economy,* Baltimore, 1820. Citations, however, will be made from the second edition, *The Elements of Political Economy in Two Parts* (2 vols.), Baltimore, 1823.

[2] *Ibid.,* vol. i. pp. 158 ff.

class of merchants with national interest, said Raymond, supposes that national wealth increases by accumulation, that is, by an excess of production over consumption. Ganilh, a belated partisan of mercantilism, therefore presents only a "partial system of political economy." Raymond tries to quiet Ganilh's fears by attacking this "partial system" with vigor. He alleges that Ganilh is mistaken in dreading the evils which might result from the separation of private wealth from public wealth. Because private and public wealth are different, it does not follow that they should flow from different sources, nor does it follow that differentiation would dry up the sources of one or the other. The whole problem is simply to discover whether the flow of private wealth is, or is not, contrary to the flow of public wealth in order to discover the advisability of modifying the flow of private wealth. To Raymond, it seemed probable that the interest of the merchant and the interest of the state were more often antagonistic than identical. The balance of trade could not be considered a sure index of the wealth of a nation because, unlike a merchant, a nation might buy more than it sells without growing poor![1]

Whatever the analogy between national wealth and agricultural wealth, the doctrines of the Physiocrats constitute also only a "partial system of political economy." They confused national interest with the interest of a particular agricultural class and subscribed to the dogmas of overproduction: a necessary excess of production over consumption.[2]

In Adam Smith, Raymond notes the decisive step made in the error. Not content with confusing the individual with the state, Smith makes abstractions of their concrete forms. Henceforth there is no longer an identification of

[1] Raymond, vol. i, pp. 166, 167, 168.
[2] *Ibid.*, vol. i, p. 84.

national interest with the interest of any one class, but an identification of national interest with individual interest in general. The nation, however, is made up of individuals; and national interest (which no longer adheres to any group but is infinitely dispersed) is absolutely reduced to nothing. Although Smith sometimes adopts the agricultural system and sometimes the mercantile, in the end he repudiates both. In doing this, said Raymond, Smith "does not suggest any system of his own, unless 'no system' be his system." A system of 'no system' is as false as the others, he insisted, and Adam Smith is either the advocate of no system of political economy, or the advocate of an erroneous system.[1]

Yet, in Raymond's opinion, the writer who exceeds all bounds is J. B. Say. Not only is his rejection of all system extreme, but his economic doctrine "the strangest doctrine of all" has for its very center the idea of over-production. The relation between production and consumption gives way completely to a consideration of the relation between production and over-production. Say, said Raymond, has not even tried to define public and private wealth. He actually confuses them respectively with property and with value. He applies the term "wealthy" as readily to a man who has one dollar as to one who has a thousand. The result is confusion, vagueness, ambiguity, obscurity and superficiality. Say's structure is still a "partial instead of a general treatise on political economy." The fundamental principles of Say's work, said Raymond, "so far as it has any, are the same [as those of the *Wealth of Nations*] but in comprehensiveness of views, and in the powers of reasoning, M. Say is vastly inferior, both to Adam Smith and Malthus."[2]

Raymond regarded Malthus as closer to the truth than

---

[1] Raymond, vol. i, pp. 63, 155, 156, 158, 161, 163, 164.
[2] *Ibid.*, vol. i, chap. vi, and pp. 172–3.

either J. B. Say or Adam Smith. To be sure, Malthus always confused individual wealth with public wealth (the latter only increasing in proportion to the increase in production). In consequence, this is still only a "partial system." Nevertheless, because of his qualifications and because of his sense of reality, Malthus' theory more closely approximates the truth.[1] Lauderdale, by the help of Malthus' sound applications, finally disentangled the logical principle by rejecting the fundamental error and thereby distinguished national wealth from private wealth. Yet he, in turn, failed to comprehend the nature of value since he failed to distinguish its technical from its ordinary meaning. The reason why gold and silver have no value among savages is because there is no opportunity for exchanging them and not because these metals are abundant. If Lauderdale had really considered the nation as a unit, he could never have supposed that the mass of individual wealth could possibly be increased through scarcity of such a commodity as water. The sum of individual wealth would remain the same because the total wealth of the rest of the community would decrease in exactly the same proportion as the wealth of the monopolists of the water springs would increase. We shall see that, for Raymond, the difference between national and private wealth is a specific difference: the difference between a productive force and the product thereof.[2] Hence the common error of his predecessors, said Raymond, was the confusion of national and individual wealth, although the degree of error varied. To the absolute doctrines of Adam Smith and J. B. Say, Raymond was definitely opposed. In setting forth his objections to these doctrines, Raymond reconciles by systematizing not only the qualifications of Malthus and

[1] Raymond, vol. i, pp. 169–70.
[2] *Ibid.*, vol. i, pp. 174–8.

Lauderdale but also the doctrines of the Physiocrats (who were wise enough not to make abstractions) and even the doctrines of the Mercantilists (who were wise enough to take cognizance of national exigencies). Meanwhile, not content with correcting the existing doctrines, Raymond made his own contribution and presented a truly original system of political economy.

SECTION IV

From the Restoration of the Individual in Economic Theory to the Economy of "Effective Labor"

From the very outset, Raymond attempts to reestablish, in his theory, the reality of the economic world by determining the variable rôle of the individual in it. The fundamental principle of every true system of political economy, said Raymond, is labor. He alleged that the various economists had either failed to define labor, or when they did make an effort to be precise, as Say did, they gave too broad a definition: a definition, which included the productive services of nature and of capital.[1]

"Labor," said Raymond, "is the exertion of human power for the purpose of producing the necessaries and comforts of life." All labor is productive. Immaterial products are included in his definition of wealth. "We are gravely told," said Raymond, "that a man who wields the spade, or throws the shuttle, is a productive labourer, while Bacon, Newton, or Washington were unproductive labourers." The productivity of labor, however, does not really depend upon its nature, but upon the realization of a purpose. In the same manner that Raymond repudiates the materialism of Smith, he also repudiates *a fortiori* the materialism of the Physiocrats. "The sophistry of those who maintain

[1] Raymond, vol. i, chap. iv.

that agricultural labour alone is productive, consists in confounding the fecundity of the earth with the labour of man, and in attributing to agricultural labour, that which belongs to the powers of nature." [1]

Does that mean that Raymond reacted against the ideas of Smith and adopted those of Say? Indeed not! For while Raymond, like Say, rejected the distinction between productive and unproductive labor, he did so by setting up a distinction between productive and "effective" labor. As contrasted with Say, he succeeds in differentiating the one form of labor from the other. Effective labor "does not cause a product, but it augments the capacity to produce." It consists of preparatory labor, scientific discoveries, and the perfection of the arts. In short, it is labor which creates capital. Raymond maintained that Say gave too broad a meaning to the term "production" when he said that "production is a creation, not of material, but of utility." To be sure production includes the provision of all the fruits of the earth destined for human consumption (as well as certain immaterial products whenever consumed as products) but it does not include the results of "effective labor," that is to say, of that production which has for its purpose the augmentation of future production rather than the creation of immediate products. On this point the doctrine of Raymond suggests the modern theory of capital. The result of "effective labor" is nothing more or less than that which we designate today as producers' capital. In the last analysis, according to Raymond, there are only two factors of production, man and nature. These factors produce wealth in two ways: either man may apply his labor directly to nature, or he may apply it indirectly. The first method is direct production: Raymond's productive labor. In the second method, man makes no demand upon nature

[1] Raymond, vol. i, chap. iv.

for a product which will directly satisfy his wants but rather for some intermediate product which will be instrumental ultimately to satisfy his wants better although indirectly. This latter method is indirect production: Raymond's concept of "effective labor." It is Robinson Crusoe, no longer catching fish with his hands, but constructing a net. It is the fabrication of intermediate goods, as contrasted with consumers' goods. In Raymond's theory, the whole mysterious force of capital is explained in terms of the productive force of labor alone. This labor force divides itself, however, into productive labor, which is labor in the narrow sense, and "effective labor," which is the creation of producers' capital. Thus Raymond, after having repudiated the Physiocrats and Smith, also repudiates Say, by substituting his own concept of a productive force (in which labor is the dominant element) for Say's doctrine of the parity of the factors of production.[1]

Raymond's reaction against Say is indeed so pronounced that he actually tends to return not only to the doctrines of Smith but even to those of the Physiocrats when he differentiates the earth as the "source of wealth," from labor which is the "cause of wealth." After having reconstructed labor as a productive factor by demonstrating that it need not create a material product, and, after having distinguished productive from "effective labor," he proceeds to subordinate labor, as a whole, to land by the distinction between the "cause" and the "source" of wealth. In doing this, to a degree he returns to the physiocratic notion. Raymond now seems to be reasoning in a circle.[2]

Raymond reproaches the various writers for failing to recognize this essential distinction between the "source"

---

[1] Raymond, vol. i, chap. iv and p. 116. Cf. also. Böhm-Bawerk, *The Positive Theory of Capital*, New York, 1923.

[2] Raymond, vol. i, chap. v.

and the "cause" of wealth. Some, he said, explain national wealth as the result of a favorable balance of trade which leads to an inflow of the precious metals; others explain national wealth as the result of agricultural labor. To some writers, national wealth is the result of division of labor and parsimonious consumption; others attribute it to the labor of manufacturers and merchants; while still others explain national wealth as the result of land, labor and capital. No two of these writers agree in suggesting the distinction between the "source" and the "cause" of wealth.

The "source" of either private or public wealth is land. But land does not produce spontaneously. "It is a law of nature that man shall eat bread in the sweat of his face." While land is the only "source" of wealth, labor is the only "cause." Labor is the "fundamental principle of every true system of political economy." Lord Lauderdale, said Raymond, is deceived in presenting land, labor, and capital as three original sources of wealth. For if the word "source" is taken in its proper sense, then labor is not a source of wealth. If the word "source" is synonymous with cause, then land is not a source of wealth. As to capital, it can only be an instrument, a means of acquiring wealth. It is neither the "cause" nor the "source" of wealth unless in this last case it consists of land.[1] The Physiocrats, said Raymond, were closest to the truth when they wrote, "let the sovereign and the nation constantly keep in view that the earth is the sole source of riches, and that agriculture is what multiplies them." It is only necessary to substitute the word labor for agriculture to render the proposition correct. The Physiocrats "represent the earth as the only original source of wealth, in which they are no doubt right; and they represent agricultural labour as the only productive one, in which they are manifestly wrong." Raymond

[1] Raymond, vol. i, pp. 122 ff.

saw clearly that Smith had never been able to liberate himself from the physiocratic influence. The only difference between Smith and the Physiocrats, he held, was the degree to which they developed the same principle.[1]

Even if the earth is the only "source" of wealth, agricultural labor, according to Raymond, is not the only productive labor. It is true that agricultural labor has qualities which other labor does not possess, and, therefore, it should not be confused with other kinds of labor. In other words, Raymond tends to approximate the physiocratic doctrine not only because he recognizes land as the only "source" of wealth but also because he admits that agricultural labor is *almost* the only "cause" of wealth. Agricultural labor, in his opinion, differs from other kinds of labor from three points of view: social, political, and economic. In this analysis, Raymond invokes the aid of his legal training. No one, he alleged, had been able to distinguish the qualitative difference between agricultural and industrial labor; a distinction which is fundamental in economic theory. He felt confident that some light could be thrown on this problem by considering the legal distinction between real and personal property.[2]

The social superiority of agriculture, said Raymond, is both moral and natural. "Agriculturalists are a superior class of men to manufacturers. They enjoy more vigorous health and possess more personal courage. They have more elevated and liberal minds. It is much more congenial to man's nature to be abroad in the fields, breathing a pure air, and admiring the works of creation, and the beauties of nature, than to be confined in the unwholesome, impure air of a workshop. The former softens the heart and liberalizes the mind—the latter hardens the heart, contracts the

[1] Raymond, vol. i, chap. xvii, pp. 370 ff.
[2] *Ibid.*, vol. i, p. 121.

mind and corrupts the passions."[1] To this moral superiority of agriculture is added a natural superiority. Agriculture, manufacture, and commerce seem to be only different forms of labor except that agriculture is the "basis of the whole." Labor which furnishes the subsistence of life is more important than labor which provides comfort. Labor which satisfies natural wants is superior to labor which merely satisfies artificial wants. For this purpose, Raymond compares the contemporaneous state of America and of England. Since the Napoleonic Wars, said Raymond, there had been over-production in both countries. There was, however, this difference that in England there had been over-production of manufactured goods, while in America, an over-production of the necessaries of life. Between these two types of over-production, Raymond signalized a great difference. America alone had profited, since agricultural products provide nourishment and subsistence, whereas manufactured goods possess for the producer only the utility of saleability. The natural quality of agricultural labor leads, therefore, to the social superiority of agriculture. We are in the habit of confusing a trade depression, said Raymond, with national misery. We constantly confuse a group of agitated and clamorous individuals in a nation with the nation itself. National distress, however, consists of a lack of the necessaries of life. A commercial depression is not the kind of distress which touches life itself. Real national distress must always be sought among the ranks of the laboring classes since misery with them is "a distress which touches life."

After having shown the social superiority of agriculture, Raymond turns next to the political aspects of agriculture. The question which presents itself to the political economist, said he, is whether or not a nation will devote itself to

[1] Raymond, vol. i, pp. 215–6.

a single branch of industry or whether it will develop all equally. In principle, it depends upon time and place. But in any case, despite the soundness of nations which provide themselves with whatsoever they need by means of international trade, it is better that a nation should be able to supply itself with food because, in that case, social justice is strengthened by political security.

Even from the economic point of view, Raymond argued that a certain superiority must be conceded to agriculture. To be sure, agriculture is no more productive than other branches of industry, but it offers the double advantage of catering to a relatively invariable demand, and secondly, of providing thereby a more steady demand for labor.[1]

Such, in Raymond's opinion, were the social, political, and economic advantages of agriculture. Not only is land the only "source," but agricultural labor is *almost* the sole "cause" of wealth. As near as Raymond now is to the Physiocrats, he cannot resist observing that although nature assists agriculture, it also assists industry by turning water wheels. As near as Raymond is to the Physiocrats, he is going to ally himself even more closely by proclaiming the dominant position of agriculture not only in production but in distribution. At this very moment when all differences between Raymond's theory and the physiocratic doctrines seem to have disappeared, at this very moment, he makes a sudden *volte-face,* and we are then able to seize, in its complexity, all the original force of his work.

The whole problem of distribution, said Raymond, is conditioned by agriculture. Since land is the sole "source" of wealth, and since agricultural labor has priority over all other kinds of labor, it follows that the product of agricultural labor is the basis of all subsequent products. The law which governs the division of this basic agricultural

[1] Raymond, vol. i, p. 134.

product must be a fundamental law underlying the partition of the products of every other species of labor.[1]

What Smith and Malthus called profits, Raymond held to be partly rent and partly wages. What they called profits of capital, said he, is either rent or interest, and, in order to avoid a multiplicity of terms, it is better to call it rent rather than interest. If the profits of the entrepreneur reduce themselves to wages, and if the profits of capital (or interest) reduce themselves to rent, only two shares remain: rent and wages. Granting the superiority of agricultural labor and granting that all distributive shares are resolvable into rent and wages, the whole problem of distribution is conditioned by agriculture.[2]

What is Raymond's solution for the problem of distribution? It is a solution quite different from the Ricardian. Rent as the price of land is determined by the law which determines the price of all other things: the law of supply and demand. According to the abundance or scarcity of land and according to the population of a country, the price of land (rent) is necessarily high or low while, conversely, the price of labor (wages) is low or high.[3]

This economic process only influences the nominal price of the product. The level of wages does not depend, however, upon the nominal price of labor, that is upon money wages, but upon the relation which exists between rent and wages; in other words, upon the partition into rent and wages of a jointly produced product. If there is an abundance of land, rent will be low. It does not follow from this that wages will necessarily be high; the land, for example, may be so unequally divided that an over-abundance of laborers will emerge. In that case,

[1] Raymond, vol. i, p. 135.
[2] *Ibid.*, vol. i, p. 134.
[3] *Ibid.*, vol. i, p. 135.

laborers cannot obtain their proper share of the product. Rent, said Raymond, obeys the general economic law of supply and demand; but it should also be subject to social law. Indeed, the social law is a third force which influences rent, and thereby influences distribution as a whole. If social inequality inclines the balance to the advantage of rent, political sagacity can re-establish the equilibrium for the benefit of wages. It is by developing "effective labor" that political authority can assure the progressive condition of a nation.

The proportion between productive labor and "effective labor" depends upon two factors. In the first place it is related to the natural situation of a country: there will be more "effective labor" in a new country than in an old. A second factor, nevertheless, overshadows the first: "If one nation is found to enjoy a greater degree of prosperity and to be more rapidly increasing in wealth and population than another, it may be taken for granted that its political institutions are the wisest and operate in such a way as to encourage the people to make provision for the future as well as the present, by directing a portion of their labor to permanent improvements, which will increase the capacity for future production."[1]

If a great number of laborers are employed in "effective labor," there will be an increase of national wealth. Wages will be high and rent correspondingly low. Laborers will receive a larger part of the total product and landowners a smaller, although the landowners will receive, in place of their full share of the total product, an equivalent in "effective labor" which will enhance the value of their land so that the increase in national wealth will largely compensate the diminution of individual wealth. To insure national prosperity, it is therefore essential that wages should be

[1] Raymond, vol. i, p. 150.

high. Raymond recognized that the development of a prosperous agricultural class would assist manufactures and *vice-versa*. If national wealth, on the other hand, is stationary, there will be but a feeble demand for "effective labor"; wages will tend to be low and rents high. This tendency would become even more serious should national wealth begin to decline.[1]

Because of the interaction above described, Raymond believed that distribution was governed by the proportion between rent and wages. It may often be difficult, he said, to appreciate this dependence; but of its existence there can be no doubt. Raymond agreed with Malthus that the best governed society is one in which agriculture and industry co-exist in a correct proportion. If one occupation should predominate, it is the duty of the government to restore the equilibrium. In the case of England, he believed that manufacturing has been over-developed; in the United States, agriculture. The idea, common to Raymond and Malthus, was that care must be taken to preserve productive harmony between industry and agriculture by means of political intervention. But whereas Malthus would admit only external political intervention, Raymond would allow internal political intervention; that is, social intervention.[2]

This analysis illustrates how Raymond attempts to re-establish economic reality by pointing out the variable rôle of the individual in production. By his rejection of the distinction between productive and unproductive labor he repudiates the materialism of Adam Smith and the Physiocrats, and appears to approximate the doctrines of J. B. Say. Yet by means of a new distinction between productive and "effective labor," he in turn repudiates Say. He

[1] Raymond, vol. i, pp. 149–50 and 216.
[2] *Ibid.*, vol. i, pp. 169–70.

accentuates this reaction against Say by his distinction between land as the "source" of wealth and labor as the "cause." In setting up this distinction he approaches nearer to physiocratic notions than did either Malthus or Smith. The resemblance between Raymond's doctrine and that of the Physiocrats lies not only in his glorification of land as the "source" of wealth but in his admission that agricultural labor is *almost* the sole "cause" of wealth. Moreover, Raymond contends that in the same way that agriculture governs production, it also governs distribution. Curiously enough, at the very moment when one is led to believe that Raymond has made a complete return to the physiocratic position, he suddenly extricates himself and reacts definitely against the Physiocrats but without returning to the doctrinal position of J. B. Say. Indeed, it is upon his concept of "effective labor" that Raymond ultimately builds his economic theory. This essential concept enables him to repudiate the reasoning of his predecessors with his own weapons, rather than by pitting one existing doctrine against another.

In brief, Raymond in seeking for a true system of political economy ranges critically through existing economic doctrines. First he moves away from physiocracy toward Say's theory, then from Say's doctrines to his own concept of "effective labor." In seeking the basis of production, he goes, conversely, from "effective labor" back toward the physiocratic idea. Yet his re-acceptance of the physiocratic theory of production is qualified, and he returns to his concept of "effective labor." In each case it is upon this concept that he proposes to build his economic theory. This concept is fundamental; it is the heart of Raymond's economic theory and of his political theory as well. We must therefore analyse the concept in detail.

SECTION V

*From the Doctrine of "Effective Labor" to a Concept
of State Intervention*

What unity or harmony can there be in an economic
theory which attempts to combine physiocratic notions
with a germ of socialism and an economy of "effective
labor"? The notion of labor, which in Raymond's theory
is the substance of national as opposed to individual wealth,
is also the understructure of his agrarianism and his socialism. But whereas the substance of national wealth is
"effective labor," the substance of individual wealth is
value. The various economists, said Raymond, by confusing national and individual wealth, were led thereby
to attach an undue importance to the problem of value.
Unlike Smith, Raymond believed there could be no other
value than exchange value and that the measure of exchange value could be neither fixed nor immaterial.[1]

Value means exchange value. Individuals exchange only
the surplus above what is necessary for subsistence because whatever is necessary for subsistence cannot have
less value than the individual's own life. Raymond agrees
with Say when he declares that one cannot speak of "value
in use" because it is impossible to refer to the value of a
thing which has not been and cannot be evaluated.[2]

Value, not labor, is the substance of individual wealth!
For this reason, labor cannot be a fixed measure of individual wealth. The value of all things varies according
to the intensity of wants. Precious metals provide the
best standard of value. To be sure, they provide only a
variable standard; but no standard of value can be other-

[1] Raymond, vol. i, chap. iii.
[2] *Ibid.*

wise, and to speak of a fixed standard of value is as absurd as to speak of a fixed standard of elasticity.[1]

Raymond was convinced that some commodity must be the basis of a monetary system. As it is impossible to measure length or weight by means of an object which has neither weight nor length, so is it impossible to measure value by means of something which has no value. Money, said Raymond, can have no greater value than the quantity of bullion it contains. He overlooks the subjective nature of the value of money quite intentionally; in fact, he prides himself on having ruled it out of account. To a certain degree, however, he comprehends money's social character. Money, he alleged to be different from other commodities for two reasons. In the first place, money can never be anything except value, not wealth. Secondly, whereas money has a private domain in which it is more absolute than ordinary commodities, it has a public trait which is peculiar to it. This public characteristic is due to the fact that coinage is a prerogative of government and hence, although money is only a standard of value, it is a legal standard.[2]

As a result of his restriction of value to individual wealth, Raymond rejects the classical belief that an increase of national wealth is the result of accumulation (an excess of production over consumption) because this belief clashes with Raymond's naturalism. In conformity with the laws of the moral world (which regulate human action) and in conformity with the laws of the physical world (which regulate production) the relation which should exist between production and consumption should be one of equality. The greatest national prosperity, said Raymond, is achieved when the whole product of one year

[1] Raymond, vol. i, pp. 64–5.
[2] *Ibid.*, vol. i, chap. xi.

is consumed in the next. All the surplus ought to go up in smoke or be thrown in the ocean. A good system of political economy should conform to the seasonal revolutions of nature. The best illustration of this great law, applicable alike to individuals or nations, is the biblical account of the manna in the desert.[1]

Even laying aside the matter of naturalism, the very essential difference between the individual and the nation would lead one to reject the classical doctrine of accumulation. For there is the same contrast between national wealth and individual wealth as between labor and value. The nation should be distinguished from the individuals who compose it, because the nation, in a sense, is immortal. Governments, said Raymond, are delegates of God upon earth, and as such should consider not only present but future interests. Unfortunately, most legislators believe that the life of the nation does not transcend the span of theirs.[2]

Raymond conceived of the nation not only beyond the limits of time, but also beyond limits of space. A nation (and especially America), said Raymond, is "as it were, alone" in the world. It is only if we place the individual upon a desert island, that we can properly identify the individual with the nation. What advantage could an individual upon a desert island gain by saving? With whom could he exchange his surplus? The only difference, said Raymond, between a nation and an isolated individual would be that the nation's population would increase in proportion to any increase in its supply of subsistence. In consequence, the nation would increase in wealth at a disproportionately slower rate than an individual would. From this reasoning, it would appear that Raymond does

[1] Raymond, vol. i, chap. vi.
[2] *Ibid.*, vol. i, chap. ii.

not regard population as a source of wealth. However that may be, Raymond saw the same difference between national and individual wealth, as between the nation and the individual. National wealth has an absolute meaning, while individual wealth has only a relative meaning. A nation can neither rent nor sell its land but must itself cultivate it. Each day, the nation consumes an amount of goods which it cannot acquire abroad. Yet why could not this supply of food be obtained abroad? Because, said Raymond, of the fundamental law of labor. The nation, "this huge artificial being is composed of millions of natural beings" to whom it has been said, "in the sweat of thy face shalt thou eat bread," and not in the sweat of another. Labor and production should replace war and spoliation. National wealth must have an economic, not a social origin, because national wealth arises out of a relation of man to things, not out of a relation between men. Herein it differs from individual wealth. Since national wealth has this economic origin, the nation is characterized less by its perpetuity than by its isolation. By isolation, Raymond meant national self-sufficiency: man's attachment to the soil and the supreme law of labor.[1]

But was not the ancient law and prophecy, "In the sweat of thy face shalt thou eat bread," made to the individual rather than to the nation? The nation, said Raymond, is only the means of imposing the observation of this law upon the individual. In reality, this natural law which was meant to apply to the whole world and to each nation is actually hindered in its application to individuals. The artificial rules of private property, which maintain inequality of wealth, permit certain persons to eat bread produced by the sweat of another. To the extent that it is necessary to apply the ancient law of labor

[1] Raymond, vol. i, chap. vi.

to individuals, social considerations outweigh national. Both the agrarianism and the socialism of Daniel Raymond find their origin and their importance in the essential concept of labor. Agrarianism is the natural relation of man to things; socialism is an artificial re-establishment of this natural relation. Yet, if labor is the foundation of both Raymond's agrarianism and his socialism, does not his concept of labor ultimately rest upon nationalism? If such be the case, is not the chief factor in Raymond's theory political rather than economic?[1]

A nationalist policy both strengthens agrarianism and fixes definite limits for it. The political body, said Raymond, can fall into a state of lethargy and torpor. It then becomes necessary to excite its energies by administering stimulants although to accomplish a desired effect, one must appreciate the cause. National wealth is the result of labor, and can increase only in proportion to the labor expended. Labor expended in war might have beneficial results; but labor expended on public works will obviously have greater results. To the extent, therefore, that the state can stimulate the industry of its population, it necessarily increases well-being: "If we were to form an opinion on this subject, from observation in the different regions of the globe, we should be led to suppose that national wealth ordinarily existed in the inverse ratio of the natural fertility of the soil, and, that the necessaries and comforts of life were least abundant and more difficult to be acquired in a luxuriant than in a sterile country. . . . Compare England with the fertile plains of South America. . . . The relative wealth of two agricultural countries, no doubt, depends essentially upon the natural fertility of their respective soils, but it depends even still more essentially on the degree of industry which prevails in the

[1] Raymond, vol. ii, p. 322.

two countries. . . . A greater degree of industry will overcome almost every disadvantage of climate and soil."[1]

Since Raymond advocated economic nationalism, he
recommended that labor (the very cause of national
wealth) should tend to become more industrial and less
agricultural. One artificial factor should lead to another.
The means of developing national industry, said Raymond,
should be the "political corporation." In spite of the teachings of Adam Smith, England and all other nations have
continued to follow a system of monopolies, and monopolies
no doubt will continue as long as the world remains divided
into separate and independent nations. Each nation ought
to consider only its own true interest, independently of
that of other nations. Little does it matter that free trade
may be more favorable to the general interest of the human
race. Well ordered charity begins at home. "At present,"
said Raymond, "the duties of government extend no farther
than to the protection of its own citizens." Every idea of
universal philanthropy he branded as "chimerical." As
to the advantage which a nation may receive from a
monopoly over her markets, it is not the profit which is
of importance, but the stimulation which it provides for
increasing national wealth by insuring stability of demand.
With regard to tariffs, Raymond therefore laid down two
fundamental rules: 1. that the tariff, instead of being reduced, should be frequently increased; 2. that the rates
should be low upon articles not produced in the country,
and high upon those which provide most employment for
domestic labor. The colonial system, so severely criticized
by the classical economists, Raymond regarded as a
monopoly which obeyed the same principles. It is only
if this system results in greater disadvantage to the colony
than benefit to the mother country that it should be aban-

[1] Raymond, vol. i, pp. 143, 150; vol. ii, chap. iv.

doned. It was therefore logical that Raymond should regard taxes and bounties more useful than disadvantageous (Smith, Ricardo, and above all, Say to the contrary notwithstanding).[1]

Whereas public monopolies ("political corporations") should be favored, private monopolies ("money corporations") should be forestalled. Here we grasp the structure of Raymond's nationalism and the germs of his socialism. At first sight, his nationalism, which would limit agrarianism by state action, seems to strengthen his socialism.

Private monopolies give one citizen an advantage over another and are consequently advantageous to the individual but prejudicial to national welfare. Likewise, public monopolies, which give one nation an advantage over another, are useful for increasing national wealth although prejudicial to foreign nations. If there were a legislature, said Raymond, designed to protect the interests of the whole world, such a legislature would be justified in suppressing national monopolies. Raymond refuses to see that public monopolies are in the final analysis private monopolies and that they are much more utilized by individuals than useful to the nation. Private monopolies, said Raymond, should be repressed absolutely, especially "money corporations" and the "banking system."[2]

The purpose of a "money corporation" is to give to its members an artificial power which they would not have had without it, or to exempt them from certain obligations to which they would otherwise have been bound. It is a means of artificial power employed by the rich for increasing their already excessive economic domination and for destroying the natural equality between men, which every government should preserve.

[1] Raymond, vol. ii, chap. vi.
[2] *Ibid.*, vol. ii, chaps. vii, viii, ix, x, xi.

As for the "banking system," it leads to a multitude of evils: monetary depreciation, usury, extravagant speculation, sudden fluctuations in prices, bankruptcies, etc. All these evils result from banks' functions of lending and note issue. The creation of a public debt, said Raymond, is to a certain extent comparable to the "banking system," except that it avoids the evils inherent in the latter. For by creating a public capital, on which a fixed rate of interest is paid, there is created a fund in which women, children, and all those incapable of active business can invest their money with profit to themselves and benefit to the public.

Although Raymond accepts the idea of capital in a technical sense, he totally rejects the idea of capital in a legal sense; that is, any separation of property from labor. In stressing national, rather than private interest, Raymond accepts the technical idea of capital. In similar fashion his nationalism determines the extent of his social tendencies.

In accordance with the principle that God has the right to deprive man of his health or his life, the government has the right to deprive him of his property. Contrary to the Malthusian theory, Raymond maintained that, with the development of artificial wants, it is unequal division of property that restrains population. The misery of the poor is not their fault, but the fault of bad government. Primogeniture must give way to equal partition of property. In case of parental negligence, the state should have the right and the duty of educating the children. Moreover, the state must provide work for the whole nation, either in agriculture or in industry.[1]

Here we see the convergence of the agrarianism, the socialism, and the nationalism of Daniel Raymond. His

[1] Raymond, vol. ii, chap. iii.

agrarianism is subordinate to political considerations and to social as well. The important question which arises is whether the political overshadow the social considerations or whether social considerations precede political.

It is intolerable, said Raymond, that half the nation should exist without work and without food in order to permit the other half to buy at low prices. If one replies that half of the nation cannot be compelled to support the other less fortunate half, this merely tends to destroy national unity by dividing the nation into classes and by considering the interests of individuals instead of considering the interests of the whole nation which is "one and indivisible." Monopoly of the national market may indeed raise the price of wheat, but this effect is more than compensated by the much greater demand for labor which follows. Yet only within national structure, is it necessary to maintain the equality of individuals. The division of the world into strongly unified nations is the means of preventing the class struggle. Clearly, Raymond's socialism is national socialism.

Is it really socialism, or only social nationalism? Is not the state after all the end rather than the means? God, argued Raymond, created man and made him subject to natural law. Men have formed themselves into nations in order to obtain power and to preserve themselves against mutual violence. As a nation, men "have a right to modify the laws of nature so as to adapt them to this artificial state of things." Raymond repudiates the fanciful theories of Condorcet and Godwin. It is precisely because national interest ought never to be sacrificed to individual interests that it is necessary to sacrifice certain individual interests to others. One must distinguish the strong from the weak. The problem is to reconcile equality of rights with inequality of capacity, because the strength of individuals is the first element of national wealth. In other words, for Raymond, there must be, and there can be, natural equality between individuals only to the extent that this natural equality conforms with artificial national laws. The nation then is the supreme end of both the agrarianism and the socialism of Daniel Raymond. Political considerations, he believed, must always govern the economic.[1] Out of Raymond's nationalism emerges his economic politics in which all economic considerations are subordinate to political.

Although Raymond believed that national prosperity demands that annual consumption should equal annual production as nearly as possible, he did not advocate prodigality and luxury as the means. The principles which govern national wealth are in perfect accord with every true principle of private economy. Luxury is as incompatible with these principles as is parsimony. On this point, said Raymond, modern philosophers have erred as did the ancient. His conception of economic structure goes beyond the distinction between the individual and the state to the idea of a unity; a definition of an economy, said Raymond, should rest upon a relation of means to end. Between political and private economy there exists such a relation that they are mutually reciprocating. The Smithian confusion of political and private economy has degraded "the dignity of the science of political economy into a paltry science of dollars and cents," although "this art [of becoming rich] can be much more effectually learnt in the counting room and the workshop, than by reading Adam Smith, Say, or Malthus . . . there is not an apple-woman in the market, who does not know its nature . . . as well as Adam Smith." Likewise, said Raymond, there is not a farm boy who does not better

[1] Raymond, vol. ii, pp. 11, 166, 167, 231, 232, 233.

understand the law of rent than Malthus or Ricardo. Because of the classical confusion, Raymond alleged that economic science has been misunderstood; that out of it has developed the "tedious length" especially of the literature devoted to value considered as the measure of both public and private wealth. Whether individuals should buy cheap and sell dear should not be decided in accordance with the thoroughly contemptible principles of private interest, but in accordance with the more noble principles of public interest. One can only expect individuals to be wise for themselves; it does not belong to them to have surveillance over general interest. This is the task of the legislator. Given their moral faults, one cannot expect individuals to refrain from importing slaves; the legislature must forbid them.

In Raymond's opinion, political economy had made but little progress. This he ascribed not only to the weakness of its scientific terminology but also to the fact that it is a moral and not a physical science: "Whether I have succeeded in cracking the shell of political economy, is for the public to determine. . . . Although I may not have succeeded in suggesting the true theory of political economy, yet I am fully persuaded that no one else has. The work yet remains to be done. The field for successful competition is yet open, and he who shall succeed in laying the true foundations of this sublime and noble science, will entitle himself to the benedictions of mankind." Then with that ingenuous presumption characteristic of new countries and distinctly contrary to the systematic doubts of old countries, Raymond added: "Whenever the true foundations of this science shall be laid, they will be laid in America. As our country has had the high honour of laying the true fundamentals of civil government, it must also have the honour of laying the true foundations of political economy. The two are essentially connected, and a thorough knowledge of the one affords great facilities for acquiring a thorough knowledge of the other." Americans, he added, do not possess greater natural capacities for political economy than the Europeans but merely greater accidental advantages. These advantages "arise out of the nature of our government and institutions."[1]

Such is, in the strict sense of the words, the *political economy* of Daniel Raymond. The basic idea of labor in its double aspect, natural and artificial, finds its place in the national idea. State action limits the simple agrarianism which Raymond inherited from the Physiocrats. State action limits also the germs of socialism which Raymond's theory includes. By his concept of nationalism, and by sanctioning state action, Raymond has reacted against classical *laissez-faire*. In the process, political considerations re-emerge; the influence of the state has been restored to economic theory.

SECTION VI

The American Origin of Raymond's Work

Raymond's economic theory has no formal origin. It was not derived from the diverging doctrines of Adam Smith; neither was it conceived as a criticism of the *Wealth of Nations*. We have seen that the central concept of "effective labor" differentiates Raymond from all his predecessors. In order to realize that this concept was original with Raymond, it is only necessary to examine the status of political economy in the United States before 1820, the year that Raymond's *Thoughts on Political*

[1] Raymond, vol. i, pp. 156, 171, 203, 205, and chap. xix; vol. ii, chap. xiv, pp. 334, 336-7.

Economy (the first systematic American treatise on political economy) was published.[1]

In 1817, thanks to Thomas Jefferson, there was published, at Georgetown, the treatise of Destutt de Tracy. Raymond seemingly was not influenced by this book. In 1819, the year before Raymond's book appeared, Ricardo's *Principles* were published at Georgetown. J. B. Say's *Treatise,* translated by Prinsep, was published by Biddle in the United States, in 1821, the year after Raymond's book appeared. In his second edition, Raymond discusses Say's theories but he changes none of his doctrines. He does not seem to have heard of the publication of Say's *Catechism of Political Economy,* which the Careys brought out, in 1817, at Philadelphia. In fact, the only book which Raymond had read carefully was an edition of Smith. The *Wealth of Nations* appeared first in Philadelphia, in 1789, and was reprinted in 1811 and again in 1818.

Can it be said that Raymond's doctrines were inspired by hostility toward England and were, as Cossa alleges,[2] a criticism of the *Wealth of Nations?* Indeed not! The analysis which we have made is sufficient to show that the purpose of Raymond's book was not merely to oppose the Smithian theories. In order to understand Raymond, one must discern the differences which existed between American economic conditions and circumstances, as

[1] Neill, C. P., *Daniel Raymond, An Early Chapter in the History of Economic Theory in the United States* (Johns Hopkins University Studies, 1897); Haney, *History of Economic Thought,* New York, 1920, pp. 350 ff.; Sherwood, Sidney, *Tendencies in American Economic Thought* (Johns Hopkins University Studies, 1897); Say, J. B., *A Treatise on Political Economy, on the Production, Distribution, and Consumption of Wealth,* Translated from the fourth edition of the French by C. R. Princeps, M. A., with notes by the translator; fifth American Edition, Containing a Translation of the Introduction by C. C. Biddle, Philadelphia, 1823.

[2] Cossa, L., *Histoire des Doctrines Économiques,* 1889, chap. xiv, pp. 462 ff.

opposed to English conditions. We shall then discover that Raymond's political economy was as absolute as that of the classical writers.

At the time when Raymond wrote, certain definite tendencies dominated the economic condition of the United States. Population was scattered and definitely individualistic; human labor was of primary importance. Virgin soils yielded increasing returns. Land was commercialized, leading to a confusion of rent and interest. Money was persistently scarce, and the question of monetary circulation was a pressing one. All these tendencies are reflected in Raymond's theory. In short, there existed in America, as Turner has said, a lack of balance between the sum of natural resources (which was the long factor) and labor (which was the short factor). In England, the situation was reversed. The English lack of factoral balance made Ricardo a free trader; the American disproportion between factors, coupled with the influence of French political philosophy, made protectionists out of Raymond and his compatriots. It was this set of conditions which made the tariff problem such an important one in American history.[1]

If Raymond's book had such a material origin, how can the slight success of his book in his own country be explained? Was it because of the general indifference toward political economy, of which Jefferson complained in his correspondence with Dupont de Nemours, and in his correspondence with J. B. Say? It seems doubtful whether there was any general indifference toward political economy. The first two editions of Raymond, the first in 1820 and the second (a dilution of the first) in 1823, totalled 1250 copies. At the same time, Say's *Treatise* (edited

[1] Turner, J. R., *The Ricardian Rent Theory in Early American Economics,* New York, 1920.

by Biddle) went through two editions, the first of 750 and the second of 2000 copies, both completely exhausted. Violently attacked by the free traders, and ardently defended by protectionist newspapers, Raymond inspired either violent hatred or ardent enthusiasm, but only of a small number of people. He had the warm approval of John Adams, Ferdinand Beasley, and Matthew Carey. He was praised for having refused "a servile homage to theories advanced in Europe under the name of political economy." When he published his later editions, the third in 1836 (two years after the Boston publication of another famous refutation of Smith by John Rae) and the fourth in 1840, Raymond elicited the praises of John Q. Adams, praises as enthusiastic as those of John Adams, who had admired the earlier editions. The fourth edition, like the third, consisted of only one volume and did not deal with the distribution of wealth.[1]

Raymond's limited success may be attributed partly to defects of methodology. In fact, it has not been easy here to present Raymond's doctrines logically. His treatise has, by no means, the beautiful coherence of the writings of J. B. Say. For example, in the first part of his treatise, Raymond deals in successive chapters with national wealth, value, and labor; with the source and the cause of wealth, with production and consumption; then he returns to national wealth in order to study rent, wages, agriculture, manufactures and commerce, profits, money, the Mercantile and Physiocratic Systems, parsimony and luxury. In the second part he deals with natural and conventional rights, pauperism, measures favorable to national industry, machines, the "banking system," monopolies and the colonial system, customs, finances, taxation and slavery. In brief, although Raymond is quite independent of Smith

[1] Cf. Neill, pp. 25 ff.

in essence, he follows Smith point by point in form, apparently presenting his system as a simple refutation, although it is quite a different thing. Yet, although the whole of Raymond's structure lacks cohesion, the detail is remarkable; crisp sentences compress his thoughts with the admirable conciseness of a jurist.

In reality the basic explanation of Raymond's work and its fate lies less in any formal reason than in the material influence of American economic conditions, and less in this material influence than in the manner in which these influences were construed by Raymond's personality. Born in Connecticut, Daniel Raymond (1786–1849) studied law in the famous school of Tapping Reeve at Litchfield. In 1814, he was admitted to the bar at Baltimore, where six years of "poring over musty law books had grown a weariness of the flesh; idleness too was irksome; and for mere diversion he set about putting on paper his thoughts on Political Economy." Thus a lawyer out of sheer distraction, without system, under the influence of European writings and American facts, set down with professional nicety "his thoughts upon political economy." Curiously enough, these facts shed light not only upon the defects and qualities of Raymond's method but also upon his very conception of political economy. The origin of the work helps us to understand the juridical and even biblical character of his work, such as placing in the foreground the ancient supernatural "law of labor." Raymond's legal training led him to emphasize the concept of a nation as a moral entity, as well as other legalistic concepts; for example, in his fourth edition, Raymond devoted thirty pages to a commentary on the Constitution. Like Raymond, other American writers on economics also concerned themselves with legal questions.

In addition to legal questions, Raymond's work, however, takes account of moral considerations. Perhaps this attention coupled with his defective method helps also to explain the small success of Raymond's book. For this moral attitude toward political economy crystallized into a struggle against individualism, into a protectionism simultaneously excessive and inadequate, and into a hatred of banks and of slavery. In brief, Raymond's social tendencies (in spite of the concessions which he makes to "money corporations" in his last edition) created irreconcilable enemies at the very period when public morality was degenerating.[1]

The general situation in the United States, at the beginning of the nineteenth century, was of such a nature that politics took precedence over economics. Nowhere does this tendency appear more clearly than in the works of Daniel Raymond. His economic ideas really grow out of his political theory and one cannot say that Raymond was influenced either by preceding or contemporary economists. The similarities that may exist between his theory and that of the Physiocrats, Ganilh, Smith, Say, Malthus, Ricardo, or Lauderdale are, by and large, co-incidences rather than direct borrowings. In fact Raymond is more original than the foregoing analysis would indicate. His work is replete with economic reality. This sense of reality is also to be found in the writings of three great economists whom Raymond did not and could not know. Although Raymond was not acquainted with the writings of these economists, his political economy is bound closer to the theories of these three writers than it is to classical economics. To appreciate Raymond's economic philosophy, his work must therefore be compared with the writings of Friedrick List, Sismondi, and Otto Effertz. Only then will

[1] Neill, pp. 23 ff.

the thoughts of the American economist emerge integrally in their triple aspects: national, social, and agrarian.

SECTION VII

The Comparative Political Scope and Influence of the Works of Raymond and List

Although Raymond was not influenced by List, can it be said, conversely, that Raymond did not influence List? Neill has shown points of contact between List and Raymond which indicate a significant liaison. List maintained, however, that he was not influenced by Raymond but simply by certain French economists of a second order such as Dupin and Chaptal. He also said that he was strongly impressed by the economic policy of Napoleon and by the industrial ruin which followed the fall of the Empire and the abolition of the Continental System.

In 1821, at the age of 22, while a refugee in Strasbourg, List planned to make an annotated translation of J. B. Say's *Treatise.* His political enemies, however, forced him from one refuge to another. As a result he came to America. If the notes which List prepared in Strasbourg were available, they would, beyond a doubt, help solve the delicate problem of the origins of List's system. Was it derived from Adam Müller, from Adam Smith, or from Raymond? Is it the result of German, English, or American influence? We do not know. But in any event French influence also played, in our opinion, a part which was not least important.[1]

German influence predominated. The termination of the Continental blockade inundated Germany with English goods, ruined the nascent industries, and injured the coun-

[1] Bellom, M., "La Source des théories de List," *Revue d'Histoire économiques et sociale,* 1909.

try at large. This disastrous result was largely due to the subdivision of internal customs administration within Germany, the absence of a central government, and the lack of an external customs system. The whole country was thrown open to foreign merchants. Von Jacob, Von Soden, and, Adam Müller became protectionists. List was compelled to do likewise.[1]

List, however, was destined to become a more ardent protectionist than his contemporaries. For instead of living under the influence of English politics, which were reacting against protection, List was led by circumstances to live in the new world. List must be indebted, therefore, if not to Hamilton and Raymond, at least to the environmental influences of American economic life. "Thus List's system," wrote M. Rist, "is the first which clearly impressed upon European thought the influence of economic experience in the new world."[2]

What part did French influence play? A very complex and significant part. In the first place, the economic and political measures of Napoleon were the causes of the temporary German economic prosperity. List's knowledge of English classical political economy was confined to the *Wealth of Nations.* His acquaintance with Smith's doctrines, however, was not direct but through the works of J. B. Say. While Lafayette (who assisted List in migrating to America) had rekindled his political liberalism in the new world, List, another sincere democrat, acquired in America a deep-rooted antagonism toward economic liberalism! List, who had steeped himself in the doctrines of J. B. Say while he was still in Europe, discovered that Say's works were as popular in the United States as they were in Europe. It is Say whom List criticizes in almost

[1] Hirst, M. E., *Life of Friedrick List,* New York, 1909.
[2] Gide and Rist, p. 327.

every page of his *Letters to Ingersoll*, which he published in Philadelphia, in 1827, in reply to Thomas Cooper's *Lectures on Political Economy*, delivered in 1826. Cooper was an independent disciple of Say. It is quite natural, therefore, that List should prefer Dupin, or Chaptal, or Say's own brother, Louis Say, to Jean Baptiste Say. When List returned to Germany (where Carey's "real free trade" had just been realized by the suppression of internal customs and by the creation of external customs) he published his *National System of Political Economy*, in 1841. In it, List crystallized an economic policy into economic theory.[1]

Very briefly, List's system seems to have been the outgrowth of a combination of German and American economic facts coupled with a reaction against English economic facts and French economic ideas. List's comprehension of French economic ideas, as derived from the writings of J. B. Say, has already been adumbrated. We shall, however, glide over this matter since it has only a relative interest as far as Raymond is concerned. There is, however, another aspect of Raymond's work which we cannot neglect. His social tendencies, concealed under his nationalism, doubtless have an entirely different importance and future; an entirely different importance, because they connect him with an author who was not influenced by American forces, an author whom Raymond completely ignored. This writer was Sismondi, who, in 1819, published his *Nouveaux Principes d'Économie Politiques*, at Paris, the year before Raymond's first edition appeared. The similarities between these two writers are striking but entirely co-incidental. The chief difference is

---

[1] List, F., *The National System of Political Economy*, London, 1904; *Outlines of American Political Economy, in a series of letters addressed by Frederick List, Esq. to Chas. Ingersoll, Esq.*, Philadelphia, 1827.

that Raymond's socialism is concealed by his nationalism, as actuality hides the future.[1]

SECTION VIII

The Comparative Social Scope and Influence of the Works of Raymond and Sismondi

In the first place, there is this general resemblance between Raymond and Sismondi that both are in many respects like Malthus. Raymond formally admits it. As for Sismondi, one needs only glance through his theory to recognize a resemblance to Malthus.[2]

Sismondi uses a concrete method: the observation of facts. He criticizes the abstract tastes of Ricardo and Say. He attempts to make a "philosophy of history" out of political economy. The object of political economy, said Sismondi, is not wealth, but man; not production, but distribution. The doctrine of the identity of private and general interest he regarded as a myth. Whatever Say may think, said he, agriculture is not a form of manufacture. Sismondi sings the praise of rural life, and extols the benefits of small landholdings. Why, he asks, should over-production cause economic crises and misery for the laborers? Because of the separation of labor and property. The cause of the evil is social. Only by challenging legal capital can one defeat the invidious influence of technical capital.

On this point, Sismondi goes beyond Malthus. The doctrinal divergence is well illustrated by the respective views of Malthus and Sismondi on population. Sismondi

[1] Sismondi, *Nouveaux Principes d'Économie Politiques, ou de la Richesses dans ses rapports avec la population,* Paris, 1819.
[2] Cf. Patten, Simon, *Malthus and Ricardo,* 1889. Cf. also Bonar, James, *Malthus and his Work,* London, 1885.

did not believe that there was an absolute excess of population in relation to subsistence. There was simply an excess of proletarians; that is, of those who have not the means of acquiring subsistence. Malthus held that the evil had a natural origin. He therefore recommended a remedy in the moral sphere. Sismondi, on the contrary, believed that this evil had a social and artificial origin and therefore demanded a social remedy.

This leads us to Sismondi's conception of political economy in the definition of which he differs not only from Malthus but from the whole classical school. Sismondi signalizes the separation of politics and economics. "While one aims at equality in the political sphere," said Sismondi, "inequality increases in the economic sphere . . . and the very same men who defend universal suffrage, also defend the modern system of production. . . . By an unnatural alliance, industrialism and the zeal for equality are united under the same flag." In the final analysis, Sismondi actually has neither a political economy nor even a social economy. He rejects the existing economy and its miseries. He sacrifices the science of economics to the art. Economics must at the same time be conditioned by social considerations (the hope of the future) and by political considerations (the heritage of the past). For this reason, Sismondi's theory is not political economy but *social politics*. Curiously enough, in politics, Sismondi was always a conservative. Perhaps it was because the classical writers favored both universal suffrage and modern production that Sismondi regarded both with equal reprobation.[1]

From this brief sketch of Sismondi's theory, several likenesses with Raymond's doctrines are at once evident: a

[1] Aftalion, A., *L'oeuvre économiques de Simonde de Sismondi*, Paris, 1899.

certain agrarianism, a certain socialism, a certain nationalism.

The similarity between the agrarian tendencies of these two writers is so striking that often one finds both writers using the same terms. For example, it is difficult to tell from the context and style of the following passage whether it is from Raymond or Sismondi: "Since agricultural labor is the only kind which is self-sufficient, it is also the only kind which can be valued without exchange. . . . The work of nature, this creative work which is done without man, but which nature does not turn to man's use, is the origin of the net product of land intrinsically considered. . . . The progress of agricultural wealth, increasing revenue most directly, gives impetus to other forms of progress which follow. . . . The economists of Quesnay's sect have carried the principle too far. They have failed to recognize any other revenue than that which has its origin in the soil and they have supposed that commerce, the arts, and industry have no other purposes than to serve the landed proprietor. We have not considered the income from land in such an exclusive manner. . . . The first source of wealth is land whose spontaneous forces, constantly employed for production, need only be directed to man's advantage. Land receives this direction from labor. Capital, employed to pay the wages of labor, is a second cause of wealth. And life, which gives the strength to labor, is the third. Thus all three have a direct relation to labor, and without labor, there can be no wealth. . . . As opposed to land, one can renew the other two sources of wealth: life, which gives the faculty of laboring, and capital, which pays wages."

In the excerpt above, Sismondi presents nearly the same reasons for the superiority of agricultural labor that Raymond does. Moreover, does not Sismondi proffer almost the same distinction between land as the source of wealth, and labor as the cause of wealth?[1] Around this distinction as a common center, other resemblances may be grouped. Sismondi recognized that as a result of the development of commerce, one person can only work for himself by working for others. Like Raymond he places the individual upon a desert island in order to compare him with society. "Labor and economy," said Sismondi, "for the social being as for the solitary, are always the true and only sources of wealth. . . . Let us suppose an isolated nation; human society itself is such an isolated nation, and everything that is true of a nation without commerce, is equally true of the human race." Other sentences are to be found which reveal a confused understanding of Raymond's distinction between productive and "effective labor." "We have said," wrote Sismondi, "that the labor which creates wealth can be mediate or immediate. . . . That which is true of an isolated person is even more true of society; past labor gives value to things capable of increasing the product of future labor."[2] From this economic philosophy of Sismondi, based upon land and labor, emerges a socialism and a nationalism strangely similar to the doctrines of Raymond.

In Sismondi's work as in Raymond's, there is the same recognition of a conflict between landed proprietors (who enjoy a veritable monopoly) and non-proprietors; a conflict which influences population and wages. There is the same rejection of landed property, entail, and primogeniture; the same condemnation of "money corporations." Finally, there is the same belief that it is the duty of social power to defend the poor against the rich. Sis-

[1] Sismondi, vol. i, chap. ii.
[2] *Ibid.*, vol. i, pp. 101–3, 150, 282, 285, 286; ii, pp. 55, 108; iii, p. 256.

mondi's theory, which is a reaction against the decline of government interference and against classical governmental abstention in internal affairs, represents even a stronger reaction against the decline of government interference in external affairs, against classical cosmopolitanism.

Individual interest and national interest, said Sismondi, do not always coincide: "The increase in the price of manufactured goods in proportion to the price of raw materials can be and often is a great national calamity. . . . It is not the profit of the manufacturer which constitutes national interest. . . . It is the benefit which the manufacturing process distributes among all the classes which have cooperated; it is the participation of all in a national income which had its origin in labor." As in Raymond's doctrine, so in Sismondi's, national and social considerations interact: "If the government should have as its purpose the advantage of any one class in the nation at the expense of another, it is the day laborers which the state should favor." Free competition, in Sismondi's opinion, was not an automatic means of inducing national prosperity: "Other qualities, other virtues seem to contribute more efficaciously to the increase of wealth as well as to the happiness of society; among these are love of order, of thrift, of sobriety and justice. These virtues are nearly always the result of political institutions." Finally, exactly like Raymond, Sismondi, in attacking Say, definitely repudiates the classical doctrine of accumulation. One piece of evidence, most indicative of the striking similarity between Raymond and Sismondi, is that Say's criticism of Sismondi would apply even better to Raymond. Sismondi exhorted employers to help laborers in their distress and thereby mitigate the hardships of machinery. But according to Say, whose position was diametrically opposite to that of Sismondi and Raymond, it is "inadmissible

to burden one part of society with the maintenance of another class." Sismondi regarded political economy as "the
science which is charged with surveillance over the well-
being of the human race." To which Say replied, "No
doubt he meant to say that political economy is the science
which should be understood by those charged with surveillance over the well-being of the human race; no doubt
governors, if they wish to be worthy of their functions,
should know political economy, but the well-being of the
human race would be compromised cruelly, if instead of
relying upon the labor and intelligence of citizens, we
should rely upon government." Sismondi still maintained
that political economy is "the science which teaches a government the true system of administering national wealth."
In replying to Sismondi, Say replies in a clear-cut way to
Raymond when he wrote, "The wealth of a nation is the
sum of particular wealth in the hands of individuals which
the government, fortunately, does not administer."[1]

In order to understand the relation between the works
of Raymond and Sismondi in their complexity, it is not
enough merely to emphasize the doctrinal similarities, such
as their agrarianism, socialism, and nationalism. It is
also necessary, in presenting these points of similarity, to
notice the respective harmony which exists between these
items and the direction in which they respectively tend.
Then we shall see that although the works of Sismondi
and Raymond are similar in doctrinal anatomy, physio-
logically they differ.

For Raymond, both agrarianism and socialism are subordinate to political considerations. Sismondi's order is
quite different. With seeming contradiction, he wrote,
"the nation is only the reunion of the individuals who

[1] Sismondi, vol. i, pp. 242, 388, 347, 395, 416; vol. ii, pp. 150,
285. Cf. also Say, *Traité,* p. 566.

compose it, and the progress of wealth is illusory if it is obtained at the expense of common misery and mortality." All of Sismondi is contained in this single sentence. The state is not an end in itself. The consequence is that Sismondi, as contrasted with Raymond, would abandon state interference in one sphere; *i.e.*, the field of external affairs. The rights of collecting customs, said Sismondi, have the bad effect of increasing manufacturing, of destroying the equilibrium between production and consumption, and of reducing to nil the natural advantages of each nation. Thus Sismondi rejects not only private monopolies, but also those which Raymond called "public monopolies." [1]

Sismondi not only repudiates state action in the sphere of external affairs, but he subordinates it to social considerations in the domestic sphere. What characterizes Sismondi's theory of the rôle of government, what makes his philosophy one of social politics, is that the purpose of the state should not be to stimulate economic conditions but to moderate them. Sismondi was not chiefly interested in production, as Raymond was, but in consumption and distribution. He repudiates Say's theory of markets and the concept of immaterial products, both of which Raymond accepted. With greater emphasis than anyone else, Sismondi points out the opposition which exists between producers and consumers, and, among producers, between employers and laborers. "National development," said Sismondi, "proceeds naturally in every direction; it is almost always unwise to stop it, but it is not less dangerous to hasten it. . . . If the government exercises a regulating and moderating action over the pursuit of wealth, this pursuit of wealth can be infinitely beneficial." [2]

Finally, turning back from Sismondi's theory of govern-

[1] Sismondi, vol. i, p. 231.
[2] *Ibid.*, vol. i, p. 385.

ment to his economic theory, we must notice that his agrarianism is closely tied up with the denominating social factor. According to Raymond, to the degree that politics affects economic conditions, industry affects agriculture. According to Sismondi, to the degree that social considerations restrict state action, agriculture is protected from the onslaughts of industry. Here we touch upon the essential difference between Raymond and Sismondi. Sismondi would decrease the rôle of the government in external affairs; he would abolish public monopolies as well as private. He would also definitely restrict the rôle of government in internal affairs. Still more important than the foregoing, Sismondi rejects, *en bloc*, both legal and technical capital, and with these he rejects the whole industrial system which he believed had ruined agriculture and thereby decreased economic well-being. Raymond, on the contrary, separates legal capital, which he repudiates, from technical capital which he defends. Sismondi, in line with the tradition which runs from Aristotle to Carlyle and Ruskin challenges legal capital in order to combat what he regarded as the mortal enemy of human economy, namely, technical capital.

Sismondi himself furnishes us with an explanation of the difference between his theory and Raymond's. He was conversant with American economic conditions. He pointed out the American want of capital, and he criticized, as Raymond did, the financial regime in the United States. As opposed to Hamilton, he criticized the American abuse of taxation and public borrowing. After having reproached the Americans for their acquisitive spirit, Sismondi wrote these remarkable lines whose significance has only increased with time: "They will only begin to recognize all the virtues, all the high conceptions, all the noble thoughts of older civilized nations, when they become, if not stationary, at least slower in their progress; when they will have acquired another purpose than that of increasing in population and acquiring wealth. When that time comes, when they will have found it necessary to moderate their exceedingly rapid development, they will suffer cruelly before resigning themselves to a slower pace. It is a grand and instructive experience upon which old nations should always keep their eyes." Yet in comparing the new world with the old, Sismondi added, "A nation is in a state of happiness so long as it finds itself in a progressive condition, so long as it can receive development in all directions at the same time. But a stationary nation is fixed in every way."[1]

The contiguity and the frontiers of European nations (as contrasted with the vast resources and the isolation of America) coupled with the deep-rooted Latin tradition on the Continent (as contrasted with insular England) led Sismondi to believe that political economy would have to yield before *social politics*, just as industry would have to give way before agriculture. English industrialism and its misery made a deep impression on Sismondi. As an historian he knew how centuries of agriculture had exhausted the soils of the old world; yet he knew also that one must not only consider the material past but also the moral. Happily, agriculture, in his opinion, compensated material exhaustion with a development of moral fibre.

SECTION IX

The Comparative Economic Scope and Influence of the Works of Raymond and Otto Effertz

While Raymond's economic politics found magnificent continuity during the nineteenth century in the works of

[1] Sismondi, vol. i, book iv, chap. i and pp. 325, 340, 426, 427; vol. ii, pp. 8, 9, 30, 31.

Friedrick List, and while his social politics (although surpassed by Sismondi) have a definite bearing upon the present, is there not also a future for his economic theory? Raymond understood what was essential in the relation of man to nature. His economics reach back not only to the Physiocrats but also to other authors distinct from the Physiocrats such as Cantillon, Condillac and Germain Garnier. By another doctrinal path, the type of economics which Raymond cherished also goes forward by way of Malthus and Cournot to Otto Effertz whose "pono-physiocratic" socialism, in its central idea, is singularly reminiscent of Raymond.[1] To begin with, there is the same admiration for the physiocratic doctrine. "Next to the pono-physiocratic school," wrote Effertz, "there has never been a school which spoke more truth than did the Physiocrats. If this school no longer exists, it is simply because there is no longer a political party for which this school would be useful." Yet Effertz, like Raymond, rejects the system which makes land the sole source of wealth. Likewise he rejects the system of Smith and Ricardo which makes labor the sole source of wealth. "Goods," said Effertz, "have two sources, two primitive factors, which are labor and land, and consequently, they entail labor and the services of land." For this reason, "the costs of *creating* goods are reducible to labor and land; whereas the costs of *acquiring possession* consist of labor alone." Effertz, like Raymond, has a love for legal distinctions (which he hoped would improve political economy). He distinguishes the generative process, involving man and nature,

[1] Cf. Effertz, O., *Le Principe Pono-Physiocratique et son application à la question social,* Paris, 1913, pp. 1, 21, 22, 46, 50, 53. Cf. also Allix, "L'oeuvre économique de Germain Garnier," *Revue D'Histoire économique et sociale,* 1918. Cf. also Condillac, *Le Commerce et le gouvernement, 1776,* pp. 72, 74, 288 ff. Also Bonar, *op. cit.,* and Loiseau, G., *Les Doctrines économiques de Cournot,* Paris, 1913. pp. 47, 55.

from the derivative process, involving man and man. Political economy should confine itself to "natural persons." As for "business houses," they are the concern of "commercial science." A "business house" can neither consume nor produce goods; it can only acquire possession. It can acquire possession only by a derivative and chrematistic process, which is to say that a "business house" can only make money or lose money. We need proceed no farther with the details of Effertz's system; enough has been presented to show the essential similarity with Daniel Raymond's theory.

Section X

Conclusion

The foregoing analysis has presented the political economy of Daniel Raymond in the strict sense of the term. His theory comprises the basic principle of labor in its double aspect: natural and artificial. This principle of labor finds its significance in the idea of nationalism. The influence of the state, excluded by classical economists, has been restored to economic theory to a sufficient degree that state action, in Raymond's theory, limits both surviving agrarianism and budding socialism. The origin of Raymond's doctrines is to be found less in a formal source than in the environmental influence of American economic conditions, and less in these environmental influences themselves than as translated by the personality of Raymond. Raymond's work did not exert any significant direct influence upon other economists. Yet by a series of remarkable coincidences, there is a surprising similarity between his doctrines and the works of List, Sismondi, and Effertz. Raymond's doctrine represents the contrast between American and European economic conditions. The consequence is two-fold: first, Raymond represents a re-action against the doctrines of the classical school; second, the form of this reaction was quite different from the form which it was to take in Europe where it represented the contrast between Continental and English conditions.

Although Raymond's work had but slight success during his lifetime, it is still read. This is the indication of its real value for all those who are able to discern in political economy something more than a science of business, something more than the technique of capitalism. Such persons will find three great ideas united in Raymond's theory; three ideas which, in turn, engaged the attention, among others, of three writers. In Raymond these three ideas are united under a veil of actuality and arranged in an order which the future will tend to reverse.

CHAPTER II

THE POLITICAL ECONOMY OF HENRY C. CAREY

SECTION I

The Predecessors and Contemporaries of Henry C. Carey

Most of the predecessors and contemporaries of Henry C. Carey were either lawyers, clergymen, or professors. Among these, Alexander H. Everett (1790–1847) and Willard Phillips (1784–1873) were lawyers. Like Raymond, both these writers developed their economic theory out of protectionist politics, and each based his theory upon a strict distinction between individual value and national wealth. Everett's diplomatic duties brought him to Europe from 1818 to 1825. Here he came in contact with J. B. Say. But whereas Say agreed substantially with Malthus that it was production of food which placed a limit upon population, Everett upheld the American principle that it was population which limited the quantity of food produced. Everett's claims to originality center around his insistence that political institutions, although not unimportant, are not the cause of all social evils. By taking this point of view, Everett takes issue with Malthus and, to a much greater extent, with Godwin and J. B. Say. Thus the young American school, from the first, declared its independence from the two great branches of classical political economy.

Phillips' contribution lay in his ability to present views similar to those of Everett but expressed in concrete forms: either historical or statistical. In this respect, he resembles

Benjamin Franklin and Henry C. Carey. In addition to
Raymond, Everett, and Phillips, many other Americans
wrote on economic subjects. Among these writers were
Due, Vail, Potter, Opdyke, Matthew Carey, Nathaniel A.
Ware, and Calvin Colton, all of whom, in a sense, were
economists. Some of these writers were lawyers, others
were botanists, travellers, or geographers, who looked
upon political economy as one of the arts with which an
educated man should be familiar. Most of these writers
regarded political economy not as a science but as an
art, indeed as a national art. Thus in 1848, Calvin Colton
(1789–1857) published his *Public Economy for the United
States*, while Nathaniel A. Ware (1780–1854) emphasized
political economy as an art when he said, "government by
circumstances is the golden rule in political economy."
There are as many political economies, said he, as nations.
The policy of the United States is protectionist, and the
two bases of its economic prosperity are: the more than
proportional return not only from land, but from population.

This first group of American writers on economics
(which is well represented by Raymond) was followed by
a second group of a new type. Among the latter were
fewer lawyers and clergymen and more professors. As
yet, however, there were no professional economists. In
the writings of this second group, no more of the realities
of American life were perceived than could be found in
the writings of Smith, Say, Ricardo, or Malthus. The
writers made contact with the factory or the farm only
in the lecture room or the library. They are the classical
American economists, born in England and of recent immigration. Among these classicists was MacVickar, who
used McCulloch's *Political Economy* as a textbook. Another representative was Thomas Cooper (1759–1840) a

fiery radical who emigrated to the United States at the age of 26 after he had allied himself with the French revolutionists and after he had written a reply to Burke. Imbued with the teachings of Smith, Say, Malthus, Ricardo, and James Mill, Cooper vigorously opposed the tariff bill of 1827. Samuel Phillips Newman (1797–1842) a pure disciple of Smith, also belonged to this group; so did Francis Wayland (1796–1865) who published his eclectic *Elements of Political Economy* in 1837. Wayland partially adopted Malthus's doctrines and although he declared himself a follower of Ricardo, he nevertheless made rent a factor in the determination of price. Henry Wethake (1792–1866) was also of this American classical school; he published his *Principles of Political Economy* in 1835, and also edited McCulloch's *Dictionary of Commerce*. Finally, there was also Marcus Wilson who in 1838 published his treatise on *Civil Polity and Political Economy*, a book largely patterned after the writings of Francis Wayland.

This partial and more formal than real submission of American economists to English classical thought was short-lived. With Jacob Newton, J. N. Cardozo and George Tucker, American writers recovered their independence. Newton definitely rejected the teachings of Ricardo and Malthus in so far as they bore on the tariff problem. Tucker, who corresponded with both Everett and J. B. Say, outlined in his *Wages, Profits and Rent* (1837) a psychological theory of value which abandoned the English point of view. The work of Henry C. Carey, more logical than Cardozo's, rejected the classical doctrines of Malthus and Ricardo together with free trade, but retained many of the doctrines of Adam Smith. Residual classical influence was thus combined with a partial return to Daniel Raymond and his school. Among the numerous disciples of Carey may be included E. P. Smith, C. Nordhoff, Horace Greeley, Stephen Colwell, William Elder, R. E. Thompson, W. D. Wilson, and lastly, Francis Bowen (1811–1890). The last writer published his *Principles of Political Economy* in 1856; a book re-edited, in 1870, under the significant title of *American Political Economy*.

All in all, the influence of Henry C. Carey was destined to be limited. Perhaps this was because he reflected the teachings of Adam Smith which he derived primarily from Say. Perhaps it was because his emancipation from the English classical school was only a return to the French classical school. John Bascom (1827–1911), for example, instead of following Carey, yielded before the classical renaissance brought about by John Stuart Mill; Amasa Walker (1799–1875) who hoped to make a "business science" out of economics, did likewise. Arthur Perry (1830–1905) was an enthusiastic disciple of Bastiat. To mention Bastiat raises at once the question of the relation of his theory to that of Carey. If Bastiat borrowed his ideas from Carey, then those American economists who followed Bastiat in reality were followers of Carey. It all hinges on the famous plagiarism.

SECTION II

Life, General Ideas, and Method of Henry C. Carey

Carey's life throws light on the form and the very foundation of his doctrines.[1] He was born in Philadelphia on December 15, 1793, and died on October 13, 1879, at the

[1] Carey, Henry C., *Principles of Social Science,* Philadelphia, 1858, 3 vols. This work definitively summarizes Carey's doctrines. Cf. also *A Memoir of H. C. Carey* read before the Historical Society of Philadelphia, by William Elder, Philadelphia, 1880.

age of 86. His father, Matthew Carey, Irish patriot and political exile, was "an ardent but irregular worker in the field of social science." While still a young man, Henry C. Carey became a bookseller and publisher. He read the books chosen for publication or for republication, and the reading of this self-taught publisher must consequently have been considerable. In 1835, after twenty-three years of active business life, he retired with a considerable fortune and published his *Essay on the Rate of Wages*. In this essay, which shows the influence of Senior, he advocated free trade and adopted the wages-fund theory. Carey made three trips to Europe, in 1825, 1857, and 1859, where he made the acquaintance of John Stuart Mill, Chevalier, and Ferrara.

Whereas Carey's first essay was essentially orthodox, in the last months of 1842, dazzled by the tariff of that year, he suddenly conceived what he believed to be a fundamental error of the political economy of Ricardo and Malthus. "In 1848," wrote one of Carey's friends, "his *The Past, the Present and the Future* was published, ninety days after its conception. This book will mark, in the history of political economy, the date of its declaration of independence." The fairest appreciation of Carey is that of Boucke; "In the United States," said he, "H. C. Carey was the first to unite with a general knowledge of natural science a deep interest in philosophy as well as originality in the treatment of economic problems. No American of the nineteenth century can claim more justly our high regard for labors well done than this zealous champion of monism. Scattered through his many volumes we find ideas on metaphysics, psychology, mathematics, physics and chemistry, biology and anatomy, ethics and logic, sociology and history, in the light of which his economic views should be read if we wish to comprehend him thoroughly. What Comte was to France and J. S. Mill to England, Carey, in a way, meant to America."[1]

Carey's conception of economic science and its method is a first proof of the accuracy of Boucke's appraisal. Like Raymond, Carey grasped the connection between politics and economics: "The system of this country being based upon the idea of entire political equality, we might, perhaps, be warranted in looking to our teachers for something different, even if not better, but if we should do so we should, in general, be disappointed. With few and slight exceptions, our professors teach the same social science that is taught abroad by men who live by inculcating the divine right of kings." With remarkable penetration Carey shows how the passage from autocratic to democratic political theory and the effect of democratic political theory upon economic conditions leads us to pass from political economy to what he calls "social science." Political economy, said Carey, is only an art, a practical art treating "of measures required for so co-ordinating the movements of society as to enable the laws to take effect." Indeed it is the social science which treats of "laws which govern man in his efforts to secure for himself the highest individuality and the greatest power of association."[2]

This elevation of political economy to the level of a social science makes social science itself merely a part of universal knowledge and moral philosophy. Political economy takes its place in the natural and the supernatural world (whose workings Carey did not wholly comprehend). Citing Pascal and invoking Remy de Gourmont, Carey proclaimed that "all science will prove to be but

[1] Boucke, *The Development of Economics, 1750–1900*, New York, 1921, p. 142.

[2] Carey, vol. i, pp. 11, 12, 14, 15, 16, 34, 39, 40, 63; vol. iii, p. 409.

one, its parts differing as do the colors of the spectrum, but producing, as does the sun's ray, undecomposed, one white and brilliant light." It seems quite likely that Carey derived certain of his economic harmonies from the philosophy of August Comte. At any rate, Carey adopted Comte's argument that the social sciences are the most recent, the most concrete, and the most difficult of all sciences. Following Comte's stages of reasoning, Carey cited classical political economy as an example of "metaphysical" reasoning. The stage in which political economy finds itself now, he said, "is what M. Comte is accustomed to denominate the metaphysical one, and there it must continue to remain until its teachers shall awaken to this fact, that there is but one system of laws for the government of all matter, whether existing in the form of a piece of coal, a tree, a horse, or a man—and but one mode of study for all the departments of it." This method should be naturalistic in the widest sense, because science is the interpreter of nature. Science wants to know what is and why. In turn, Carey calls to mind the cartesianism of the Physiocrats, the biology of Say, the psychology of Tarde, the sociology of Comte and Durkheim. Society is compared sometimes to the Himalayas, sometimes to the vegetable world, sometimes to the human body. History and geography furnish a multitude of examples taken from all times and all places. In comparing various nations, contemporaneously, one with another, said Carey, we obtain results exactly similar to those acquired in tracing back the centuries of history. While Carey, benefiting from the experience of the early colonists and from the social experiments of a new country, often resorts to Robinson Crusoe illustrations, he is less exclusively American in method than Raymond. Although he does not have Raymond's power of analysis, he takes a more ample view of things. His mind, essentially systematic, binds and rebinds the divergent parts of his doctrine.[1]

The amplitude of Carey's conception and of his method gives a grandeur to "social science." For this science has no longer for its purpose a mere increase of wealth (as materialistic classical political economy had) but human happiness. Social science is also a moral science. Unity does not exclude order and classification. Nature is the result of a divine plan by virtue of which man is the king of creation.

In brief, we are here in the presence of a social system. From this system, whose weaknesses are more apparent than real, we derive the essential contribution of Carey. Having grasped the social trend of political evolution as well as the influence of political evolution upon economic evolution, Carey abandons the old form of political economy and attempts to supplant it by a rather vague sociology in which economic phenomena are treated as social phenomena. It is the substance of this sociology which we must now consider.

SECTION III

The Subordination of Political Considerations to Economic

The system which Carey praises he designates as "Commerce," giving the word the connotation which it had in France during the eighteenth century: an ideal ensemble of social relations. Man, said Carey, has four characteristics which distinguish him from the animal: 1. the need of association, 2. individuality or personality, 3. responsibility, 4. capacity for progress. Association and individ-

---

[1] Carey, vol. iii, chap. xlvi. Cf. Especially, his refutation of Malthus and Ricardo, vol. i, p. 40.

uality exist in direct proportion to each other, in the moral world as in the material. Decentralization implies the development of both. Centralization is a particular manifestation of gravitation, in direct ratio to mass and in inverse ratio to distance. If men do not group themselves upon any single spot of land, it is because of the very simple reason that the stars themselves, instead of agglomerating, preserve decentralization around a particular center of attraction. Carey cherished association based upon the division of labor, a concept of organic solidarity which was also to become that of Durkheim. "It is difference," said Carey "that leads to association. The more perfect the organization of society, the greater the variety of demands for the exercise of the physical and intellectual powers—the higher will be the elevation of man as a whole, and the stronger will be the contrasts among men." [1]

As to the responsibility of man to his fellows and to his Creator, it is derived from simultaneous development of association and individuality "in the direct ratio of the approach of social government to the system under which the marvelous harmony of the heavens is maintained." Here emerges clearly the absolute monism of Carey which blends the natural and the supernatural and which makes the individual or the social group only a reflection of the unified whole. Carey argued that the slave, the soldier or the pauper is each outside the beneficence of association and of individuality. Consequently, these members of society have no responsibility whatever, because association and individuality are inseparable and lead to responsibility. Only the fourth characteristic which separates man from animals remains to be considered: man's capacity for progress. In the same way, said Carey, that mate-

[1] Carey, vol. i, p. 57.

rial progress is the result of movement (which is caused by the ceaseless decomposition and recomposition of matter) so social progress is the result of the process of association (which is caused by the decomposition and recomposition of human forms): "Were the reader now to ask himself to what it was that he had been indebted for being the man he is, his answer would be that it had been to his power of association with his fellowmen of the present, and with those of the past who have left behind the records of their experience." Carey therefore defines social science as "the science of the laws which govern man in his efforts to secure for himself the highest individuality and the greatest power of association with his fellowmen." In short, to speak of individuality is to speak of association, while to speak of the development of individuality through association, is to speak of progress and responsibility. Finally, the concrete form in which these four features are blended is social decentralization.[1]

The concept of association can best be appreciated by contrasting it with its opposite. Association, in Carey's opinion, is the mainspring of "commerce": association through the division of labor. But as association is the very opposite of anarchical isolation, so is "commerce" diametrically opposed to "trade." The characteristic of "commerce" is stability, while trade, which is essentially spasmodic and which should only be the instrument of "commerce," perverts both "commerce" and man, so that they become mere means to trade's own vicious ends. The upshot is that in the same way that "commerce" is correlated with the establishment of local centers, "trade" is correlated with "centralization." The primary end of "trade," moreover, is external. Whereas "commerce" seeks to increase domestic intercourse by the improvement

[1] Carey, vol. i, pp. 42, 43, 54, 55, 56, 57, 58, 60, 61, 62, 63.

of rivers, construction of ports, building of canals, etc., "trade," regarding such expedients with disdain, measures the prosperity of a country by the extension of its relations with distant peoples. At no time, said Carey, writing in 1858, has the domination of these forces of "trade," external to a nation, been as strong as at present. The value of all property and all labor, he alleged, followed the variations of European politics. Since he regarded imperialism as "trade" raised to a political system, Carey repudiated imperialism in favor of a wholesome protectionism whose negative purpose should simply be to protect national economy from the influence of external politics. What Carey wished to realize was "real freedom of trade": that is, the power of a nation to maintain, directly with the whole world, commerce of such a nature that that nation could substitute finished commodities as exports in place of raw materials as rapidly as the development of the division of labor within that country would permit.

Pure politics seemed even less dangerous to Carey than the contemporaneous subversive economic policy; imperialism more innocuous than economic imperialism: "The morals of war and of trade are the same. The warrior rejoices in deceiving his antagonist, all being fair in war. . . . In both, the end is seen to sanction the means— the only test of right being found in success or failure. Pre-eminence of soldiers and traders may, therefore, be regarded as an evidence of barbarism." The only difference between wars of conquest and wars designed to protect trade monopolies is simply that the violence of the latter is much greater. Even the United States, Carey deplored, was oppressing its weakest neighbor, the Mexican Republic and the poor remnants of native tribes. But the nation which had made a perfect political system out of "trade" was definitely England. The "colonial system" (in

Carey's opinion the very cause of the American Revolution) had as its chief objects the stoppage of the circulation of goods within a colony, a forced exportation of raw materials, and a forced importation of manufactured goods; in brief, a forced "trade." The distinction between political imperialism and economic imperialism is duplicated in Carey's distinction between political centralization and trade centralization. Political centralization implies a central power and heavy taxes, but it favors the productivity of labor: the source of public revenue. The primary effect of trading centralization, on the contrary, is the stoppage of the domestic circulation of goods, which in political centralization is only an incidental effect. The "trader" wishes to keep the buyers apart from each other. Personal taxes are arranged to outweigh land taxes, indirect taxes to outweigh direct. The slower the circulation of goods, the higher are the tax levies of the government. As the value of land and of labor (which should be the chief contributors to national revenue) falls, the more fraudulent the imposition becomes. This aspect of Carey's doctrine singularly recalls the teachings of the Physiocrats.[1]

Carey therefore argued that the goal of economic imperialism is realized by means of internal, anti-democratic centralization. The history of the world, he said, is replete with the machinations of strong minorities designed to restrain the increase of the power of association and prevent the proper economic organization of society. Those who govern exploit the nation instead of serving it; permanent well-being is constantly sacrificed to "trivial" and temporary profit. Among individuals as among

[1] Carey, vol. i, pp. 199, 210, 213, 214, 216, 217. Not only does Carey's theory on this point recall the Physiocrats but it suggests the single-tax of Henry George.

peoples, "trade" generates demoralization and corruption both political and judicial in proportion to the decline of the spirit of association. When the gain of one person is derived from the exploitation of another, the gain of one is sought in the ruin of another. At this point, Carey, like Raymond, invokes a great biblical law. It is not, however, the prophecy that man must eat bread in the sweat of his face; it is an ethical relation between men rather than a relation between man and nature; a social rather than an economic rule. Individuals and nations, said Carey, should do to others as they would have others do unto them. This is an idealization of the law of markets. Carey recognized, however, that the hope of realizing this maxim was remote. Politics, said he, is only the instrument of the class that lives by appropriation. The economic imperialism, which Carey decried, he alleged had a double effect upon a nation's domestic economy: monopolization of land and stagnation of agriculture. The substitution of "trade" for "commerce" he believed was correlated with a consolidation of land ownership. When any community is living from its powers of appropriation, rather than from its powers of production, it goes through a period of apparent energy. Basically this is not national economic strength, but weakness, because while centralization may enrich a minority, it can only impoverish the masses. For example, the geographical separation of the centers of production and consumption increases the necessity for transportation. These expenses of transportation (which increase in geometric proportion as the distance from the market increases arithmetically[1]) tend to become the heaviest tax which agricultural laborers have to pay. In words which remind one of Adam Smith, Carey then remarks that if human institutions never deviated from

[1] Strangely reminiscent of Malthus.

natural inclinations, cities would never increase in population beyond the number of people whose subsistence
could be furnished by the adjacent agricultural land. Men
would then be liberated from the tyranny of "trade" and
could enjoy the delights of rural life and the serenity of
mind which only rural life can foster.[1]

The sinister effects of "trade" upon agriculture lead
Carey from legal and political considerations to economic;
from politics to economics. "Trade" rests upon an inversion of end and means. An external goal (economic imperialism) is obtained by means of an anti-democratic
internal policy of centralization. The multiplication of
intermediaries, induced by economic imperialism, instead
of knitting together association, tends to dissolve it. Whatever may be the bearing of the biblical law which Carey
invokes, association, in his mind, is less a relation between
men than a relation between men and things; an economic
phenomenon rather than a political. Real association, said
Carey, is the foundation of the division of labor. He could
conceive of three chief forms of economic activity, resulting respectively in "changes of place," "changes of form,"
and "vital changes in the forms of matter." In passing
from "trade" to "commerce," national economic activity
would also undergo change. "Changes of place" would
give way to "changes in form," and "changes in form" to
"vital changes in the forms of matter." But to what extent should industry yield precedence to agriculture? Only
to the extent, said Carey, that it is useful for the realization of ideal "commerce." Carey subtly combines the law
of markets with Comtean classification and from this
curious combination he concludes that it is precisely because an agriculture stage is superior to an industrial
stage in a nation's history, that it is posterior in time. The

[1] Carey, vol. i, pp. 221, 238, 239.

logical subordination of industry results in the chronological subordination of agriculture to industry.[1]

The development of agriculture is therefore in inverse proportion to the development of "trade"; inversely proportional to foreign commerce; directly proportional to domestic commerce. The more agriculture borrows from the soil, the more fertilizer it can return to the soil, providing the producer is not far removed from the consumer.

The second characteristic trait of land is that land is a lender. This is the Virgilian quality: *"justissima tellus."* Land, said Carey, is "the great labor saving's bank," and the value of all other things is in direct proportion to their usefulness in helping man to increase his deposits in this unique bank whose dividends constantly increase and whose capital also increases. Land will give man nothing unless the debts to it are repaid, but if the debts are regularly repaid, each subsequent loan is made upon a larger scale. Carey argued that to suppose that land, in addition to the repayment of man's debt to it, demands still more capital, was an error into which the great English landlords had fallen.

Because land has been likened to industry, people have not taken cognizance of the third characteristic trait of agriculture: that agriculture is the supreme art and science. It is the grand pursuit of man! Consider, said Carey, the peaceful and intelligent character of the agriculturalist! To till the soil requires a high degree of knowledge. Physics, geology, chemistry, meteorology, electricity, entomology, vegetable and animal physiology: all these sciences are essential to the good agriculturalist. For the work of the agriculturalist is to guide the various forces of nature in order to produce the "vital changes" to which we owe the abundance of wheat, wood, sugar, rice, without

[1] Carey, vol. i, chap. x.

which neither population nor commerce could increase. Turning again to Comte's classification, Carey transports it to another sphere; agriculture becomes, in his opinion, the essence of "social science." As man grows in intelligence, said Carey, intellectual faculties supersede physical strength. Man penetrates natural laws, going from the abstract sciences such as physics, chemistry, and physiology to the more concrete. The highest of these concrete sciences and the last to develop is agriculture, because it requires a knowledge of the other abstract sciences. Likewise, of all man's activities, the last to be developed is scientific agriculture, and of all citizens, the last to be emancipated are the tillers of the soil. Carey alleged that hitherto agricultural labor had been considered as an occupation fit only for slaves. It is not slavery, said he, which causes the exhaustion of the soil, but exhaustion of the soil which has made slavery persist. For Raymond, it was bad political conditions which led to bad economic conditions; for Carey, it was just the reverse. Integral progress, said he, will only be achieved when it is recognized that the supreme science is knowledge of the delicate mechanism with which nature works. Yet high as this knowledge ranks as science, it also depends the most upon natural and social occurrences. In this sense, it is the supreme art.[1]

The foregoing scientific gradation (a transposition of Comte's law) leads to the conclusion that although logically agriculture precedes industry, chronologically it is later. For in the same way that simple and abstract sciences develop first, the simple and abstract occupations (trade and war) emerge first. Industry, consisting of

[1] Carey, vol. i, p. 221; vol. ii, pp. 24, 25, 26, 27, 28, 29, 34, 35. Cf. also Nourse, E. G., "The Place of Agriculture in Modern Industrial Society," *Journal of Political Economy*, June, 1919, March, October, 1920.

"changes of form," (mechanical and chemical changes)
comes next and necessarily makes its appearance before
the agricultural stage. Agriculture can only emerge last,
since it is the pursuit which provides the greatest good
for the mind, the morals and the heart. It is the substitution of industry for "trade" which first makes agriculture
something more than exportation of soil and natural resources. Agriculture and industry should consequently be
combined, because agricultural progress is bound up with
industrial progress. The greater quantity of food that can
be obtained from a given area of land, the greater the
number of people who can live together and conversely.
Moreover, as industry becomes more and more mechanical,
the proportion of a nation's labor devoted to it tends to
decrease; while, conversely, the proportion devoted to
agriculture tends to increase. Hence "commerce," as contrasted with "trade," does not consist in the exportation of
raw materials but in the exportation of finished commodities which have resulted from a combination of industry
and agriculture. This praise of fabricated exports is not
the only mercantilistic trait of Carey's doctrine. His
monetary theory likewise recalls to a certain extent the
ideas of the seventeenth and eighteenth centuries. However that may be, Carey believed that industrial products
had the double merit of replacing agricultural commodities
in foreign trade and thereby stimulating a nation's agricultural production. Was not this the doctrine of Cantillon?[1]

In short, Carey's political economy which oscillates between physiocracy and mercantilism consists of an harmonious juxtaposition of agricultural production and a
domestic economic policy, on the one hand; of industrial

[1] Cf. Pirou, G., "La Théorie de la Valeur et des prix chez W.
Petty et R. Cantillon," *Revue D'Histoire économique et sociale,*
1911. Cf. also Dubois, *Histoire des doctrines Économiques,* 1903.

production and an external economic policy, on the other. External industrial policy, however, is subordinated to a domestic agricultural policy; political considerations are subordinated to economic.

SECTION IV

The Theory of Economic Policy

The substitution of "commerce" for "trade" Carey thought would accomplish real association based upon the division of labor. It would decrease "changes of place" and increase "changes in form" and "vital changes in the form of matter." "Commerce" would be characterized by the advent of state action no longer centralizing and imperialistic, but simply national, defensive, and almost social. "Commerce" would initiate an economic policy which would combine industry with agriculture (subordinating the former to the latter). This economic policy would overtop political considerations so that agriculture, rather than industry, would become pre-eminent. From this intended dominant position of agriculture we cannot however conclude that, in Carey's theory, land outweighs labor as a factor of production. We must first investigate his ideas not only concerning the source of value but concerning the nature of value itself. Since, in Carey's theory, political considerations are subordinate to economic, we must discover the essential elements of value within the economic sphere. In the economic sphere, association is based upon the division of labor (which is re-inforced by technical and mechanical progress). Association not only links production and consumption geographically, but also in a time period. As a result, there is a direct geographical drawing together of production and consumption, and also an indirect economic *rapprochement*. There are three steps in this process.

In the dynamic theory of value, which Carey outlines, there is a tendency for the price of products to fall and for the price of services to rise, a tendency for these respective prices to be drawn nearer together. Carey, it is true, does not use the word "services" but speaks only of the labor and of "raw materials." Value is defined as a measure of resistance to be overcome before one can enter into possession of a desired thing. Since value is the measure of the power of nature over man, the utility of a commodity is the measure of the power of man over nature. Value, said Carey, is measured not by the cost of production, but by the cost of reproduction. To say that value diminishes is to say that the power of nature over man diminishes equally, and that conversely the power of man over nature increases. In fact, even the value of man increases, measured by the cost of reproduction. This increase in the value of man, in relation to things, constitutes wealth. For wealth is not confined to material things, but is the power to command the gratuitous services of nature. "We are accustomed," said Carey, "to measure the wealth of individuals or of communities by the *value* of the property they hold; whereas wealth grows, as we see, with the decline of values which are only a measure of the resistance to be overcome before similar property or commodities, can be reproduced. This view might, therefore, seem to be in opposition to the general idea of wealth, but when examined, the difference will be seen to be only apparent. The positive wealth of an individual is to be measured by the power he exercises; but his relative wealth, by the amount of effort that would be required to be given by others before they could acquire similar power." Carey's distinction between positive and relative wealth recalls

Say's natural and social wealth; it recalls the "wealth of enjoyment" and the value theory of Saint-Chamans; it reminds one of Bastiat's relative and effective wealth, which in turn recalls Raymond's "effective labor." [1]

Carey maintained that the diminution of the spread between the prices of the fundamental raw materials (land and labor) which tend to rise, and the price of finished products, which tends to fall, is the only essential characteristic of civilization. Hides, which formerly sold for five cents a pound and produced leather which sold for twenty cents, would now sell for seven cents a pound and produce leather at fourteen cents. Among civilized people, as contrasted with savage people, raw materials are dear, while finished products are cheap. As a result of this change in price harmonies, the structure of society changes from an inverted pyramid to a pyramid with firm foundations. Intermediaries should not be classed with agriculturalists; *i.e.*, among the producers, since they do not create wealth, but only create value. With economic progress, the intermediaries will tend to disappear. The agriculturalists will profit in two ways from the new price movement: first, by an increase in the quantity of products which they sell; secondly, by an increase in the exchange power of each of these products. Meantime, what the agriculturalist sells for a higher price, the artisan will be able to buy for a lower price than formerly. For association, based upon the division of labor, and strengthened by the technical progress of machinery, leads to a real diminution of value and an absolute increase of wealth. Carey delights in the prospect! Improvement of cultivation will tend to raise the price of land while lowering the price of wheat; improvement of methods of converting wheat into flour will tend to raise the price of wheat while lowering that of flour. Each product

[1] Carey, vol. i, chaps. vi and vii.

will be affected by both the forces of "attraction" and "counter-attraction." At each stage of the process the spread between prices diminishes: the price of land is drawn nearer to the price of wheat, the price of wheat is drawn nearer to the price of flour, the price of flour nearer the price of bread. But labor and land, these supreme raw materials of production, cannot be produced cheaper. They seem to escape the counter-attractive force and seem constantly to rise in price. Man and land, said Carey, hold fast to one extremity of the scale and finished goods to the other. The former increase constantly in value in relation to the latter —"Land, as the throne of man thus rises with his sovereign." The upshot is that although the increase in value of any given product is more or less neutralized by a decrease in the value of a subsequent product, labor and land seem to undergo only an increase of value without any corresponding diminution.[1]

Not only does the price of labor and land rise in comparison with the price of finished products but also in comparison with the price of intermediate products. Thus labor and land rise in comparison with the price of capital. This is the second step in the drawing together of producer and consumer. This decrease in the spread between the price of products and the price of services represents a drawing together of production and distribution, and also a drawing together of production and consumption. The rise in the price of services represents a rise in incomes. Increased incomes lead to a greater power of consumption. Although confused, the doctrine of economic equilibrium appears in Carey's theory. As the price of services rises in relation to the price of products, consumption surpasses production in theoretical importance. For the prices of land and labor which on the one hand increase, and the price of capital

[1] Carey, vol. i, pp. 428, 433.

which on the other hand decreases: these two sets of prices are drawn toward each other. Production, in Carey's theory, is consequently not only subordinate to consumption, but the very meaning of production, we shall see, is qualified.

The concept of capital connects production and consumption in Carey's theory. Actually production and consumption are so intermingled that it is difficult to see where one begins or the other ends. Thus sustenance is consumed in the production of man; man is used up in the production of the bow or the canoe. The canoe or the bow, in turn, is consumed in the production of sustenance. Moreover, sustenance does not cease to be capital when it has been consumed, because "man is capital"; indeed, he is the highest form of capital! Carey's concept of capital is quite flexible. Capital is "the instrument by means of which is acquired that mastery . . . over nature which constitutes wealth." This instrument might be a bow, a canoe, a ship, a mill, food, land, or human strength. Capital is not a mass of money, but a technical means of labor. Hence, the source of capital is not saving. The only concession which Carey would make to saving was that capital is a saving of human effort resulting from contrivance and the division of labor. Capital has been reduced to labor; therefore, land and labor, it appears, are the two sole and supreme factors of production. The reduction of capital to labor is also reflected in distribution. When fixed capital supplants circulating capital, as the proportion of circulating capital diminishes in relation to fixed capital, the circulation of land tends to increase. As a result, property, originally personal and moveable, tends to take the form of real property. By entering into circulation, land tends to increase in value. Capital, as a factor of production, is superseded by land, because to the extent that capital is fixed, it is absorbed by land. To an even greater extent does capital give way to labor and the power of capital over labor declines. Contrariwise, the reproduction of capital by labor becomes more and more easy. As a result, capital becomes the great levelling force. The income of labor increases in two ways: labor receives an increased proportion of an increased quantity; the share of labor, which in relation to interest was as 1 is to 2, now assumes the ratio of 2 : 3. The share of capital increases absolutely, but diminishes relatively. The laborer becomes master of the accumulations of the past. He becomes himself a capitalist. This, said Carey, is why capital increases when wages rise, and diminishes when wages fall.[1]

We have now analyzed the major part of Carey's theory of "commerce." Carey's monetary theory is, however, the synthesis of his whole doctrine. Although capital is not necessarily money, on the other hand, money is capital. In fact, Carey considered money as capital of a superior kind. Changes of place, which characterize "trade," and changes of form, which characterize industry, should give way to "vital changes in the form of matter." The exchange of services which money achieves is quite a different matter. Thanks to money, all loss of labor (the most perishable of products) can be avoided by immediate conversion: that is, by converting labor into money. Thanks to money, the product of labor can be divided without limit between the members of society. Improvements in methods of transportation are advantageous to man, but the services they render when compared with their cost are small. With money it is quite different. To be sure, money satisfies no direct want, but it satisfies an indirect want of first importance. A wholesale suppression of ships, said Carey, would scarcely affect social life, while the suppression of money

[1] Carey, vol. iii, pp. 18, 19, 20, 48, 49, 50, 51, 53, 59, 60, 62.

would put an end to social life. Providence has furnished
us with money in the form of the two metals, gold and
silver. Money is to the social body what air is to the
human. "Of all machinery in use among men," wrote
Carey, "there is none that exercises upon their actions so
great an influence as that which gathers up and divides and
sub-divides, and then gathers up again to be on the instant
divided and sub-divided again, the minutes and quarter-
hours of a community. It is the machinery of association
and the indispensable machinery of progress."

Such is the neo-mercantilism of Carey: a confused but
broad view of the social functions of money. Since money
has social functions, Carey regarded an increase of money
in any form as always desirable. This thesis leads Carey
to reject both the quantity theory of money and Gresham's
law. The index of national prosperity is to be found not
in the quantity of money, but in the rapidity of circulation.
A super-abundance of money is impossible, said Carey, for
two reasons: metallic money cannot be super-abundant
because of the non-monetary uses of the metals; paper
money cannot be super-abundant because of the infinitely
increasing number of man's wants. All this is logical if
one remembers that for Carey the value of money does not
depend upon its quantity, but upon the value of land and
labor. The value of land and labor in turn depends partially upon the quantity of money. In other words, it is
because money, by increasing in quantity, increases the
value of land and labor that it can, by that very means,
increase its own value. Carey then recapitulates his monetary theory in a final harmony. The precious metals leave
countries whose soil is exhausted, and migrate to countries
where the soil is improved. Importation of finished commodities and exportation of raw materials lead necessarily
to an efflux of precious metals; conversely, importation of

raw materials and exportation of finished commodities leads to an influx of money. The metals leave countries where money is scarce and interest rates high, for it is when money is cheap in terms of interest that it is dear in terms of finished goods. Thus Carey's whole doctrine is epitomized in his monetary theory. Although an increase in the quantity of money leads to a rise in the price of land and of labor, represented by corresponding decline in the value of money, it produces a decline in the price of manufactured goods, denoted by a corresponding increase in the value of money. "Such is the great law," said Carey, "governing the distribution of labor's products. Of all recorded in the book of science, it is perhaps the most beautiful—being, as it is, that one, in virtue of which there is established a perfect harmony of real and true interests among the various classes of mankind." In a word: the more the prices of raw materials and of finished commodities are drawn toward each other, the smaller, necessarily, becomes the proportion of the products of labor taking the form of profit, interest, freight, or rent.[1]

The theory of decreasing rent and the consequent rejection of Ricardian economics is a striking feature of Carey's work. Yet how can one reconcile the theory of decreasing rent with the constant increase in the value of land? In the final analysis, land is not a supreme factor of the same rank as labor. It is only similar in that it escapes the whole "counter-attractive" force in the price process. Like labor, it increases in value in relation to products, but in relation to labor itself, it decreases in value. This is the third step in the drawing together of producer and consumer. Neither capital nor land are ultimate factors of production. Only labor remains as the supreme factor of production and

[1] Carey, vol. ii, pp. 293, 296, 297, 298, 300, 305, 306, 308, 311, and 323–479.

the chief force in consumption. Indeed, to the extent that technical progress is fully operative and succeeds in lowering the reproduction costs of industrial products, land increases in value as labor also does at the same time. But to the extent that technical progress, which has arisen from division of labor and from the use of machinery, is applied not merely to industrial pursuits but also to agriculture, to this extent, land is affected by the normal forces outlined in Carey's value theory. Labor alone escapes the "counter-attractive" force of the price process, and, in the constitution of labor, mental force supersedes physical strength. This conclusion concerning the exclusive position of labor is not invalidated by the fact that two fields, upon which similar quantities of labor have been applied, produce products of unequal value. The same thing is true of a multitude of things whose value, without question, results from labor. Two horses, for example, after having received the same care, may have different values. In seeking to refute the theory of rent, Carey actually widens it![1]

In briefest form, this is the political economy of Henry C. Carey. It consists of an harmonious juxtaposition of agricultural production and a domestic economic policy, on the one hand; of industrial production and an external economic policy, on the other. External industrial policy should be subordinated to domestic agricultural policy; political considerations should be subordinated to economic considerations. From this pre-eminence of agriculture over industry, we cannot, however, conclude that land as a factor of production has priority over labor. For passing from the source of value to value itself, we have seen that association, based upon the division of labor (which is quickened by mechanical and technical progress) not only links production and consumption geographically but

[1] Carey, vol. iii, chap. xlii and vol. ii, pp. 268 ff.

also in a time period. There are three steps in this process. The price of finished goods falls as compared with the price of services; the price of intermediate products falls as compared with the price of services; and lastly, the price of land falls as compared with the price of labor.

Section V

The Transition from Raymond to Carey: A Weakening of the American Reaction against the Classical School

The relation between land and labor is clearly the heart of Carey's theory. Even if it can be shown that there is no contradiction between Carey's theory of rent and his theory of value, another delicate question arises. If the increase in the value of land, relative to that of products, is neutralized by the diminution of the value of land, relative to that of labor (value being always defined as the power of nature over man) in what sense can one speak of an increase in the value of human labor? The answer to these questions will be furnished us naturally as we proceed to vivify what has thus far been only pure theory with the circumstances and ideas which inspired it.

It is customary to connect the name of Carey with that of List, although Carey's protectionist theory is not as substantial and as well considered. Carey's theory, moreover, comprehends not only industrial but agricultural protection and holds itself out as a permanent system. This is an indication that Carey, who had read List's work, drew his inspiration not so much from List as from facts; from the marvelous growth of the United States (for which the tariff seemed partly responsible). Yet to the extent that List's theory coincided with the economic practice of the United States, was it not this American economic policy which List interpreted? Was not this policy also the doctrine of Daniel Raymond, a writer who definitely exerted an influence on List. One writer has correctly said: "It seems wholly probable that List was indebted to Raymond, which throws light on the vexatious question of knowing whether Carey was indebted to List. Both Carey and List borrowed from the same American source." The truth is that List is much nearer to Raymond that Carey is to List.[1]

There are many points which are common to Raymond and to List, perfectly clear in these respective writings, but which appear in Carey's works in a more or less obscure way. Among these are the criticism of the classical confusion of public with private matters, of the nation with humanity; the criticism of the principle of the identity of private and general interest; the idea of the nation as an entity distinct from the individuals who compose it and from surrounding nations; the contrast between productive forces (the substance of national wealth) and exchange value (the substance of individual wealth). Another illustration of the similarity between Raymond and Carey is found in the doctrine of "effective labor." Raymond's concept of "effective labor" makes wages a more important distributive share than rent. Carey likewise gave priority to wages at the expense of rent. But the two writers look at the problems from different points of view. The political art, so pure and vigorous with Raymond, disappears before "social science" in Carey's works. The consequences of this transition of view-point are many. With Carey it is no longer bad political conditions, but bad economic conditions which lead to slavery. With Raymond an external industrial policy was of greatest importance; with Carey it is a domestic agricultural policy which is most important.

[1] Gide and Rist. *Histoire des Doctrines Économiques.* Cf. also Sherwood, *Tendencies in American Economic Thought,* and Neill, *Daniel Raymond.*

It is quite symptomatic, therefore, that Carey should call his protectionism "real freedom of trade." The kernel of Raymond's philosophy was production; the center of Carey's philosophy was distribution. Raymond approached the Physiocrats by his analysis of agricultural production; Carey approaches them by his rejection of "trade."

Likewise, the relation of the two writers to mercantilism was different. Carey does not consider the gap separating the nation and the individual with which Raymond was so much concerned. Carey remained a convinced partisan of the balance of trade. Of economic liberalism, Carey said, "Were all this asserted of an individual man, it would be regarded in the highest degree absurd; yet it is here asserted of nations, as though the laws which govern communities of thousands and millions of individuals were not the same with those that govern each of the men of whom they are composed." This reduction of national to individual interest is the foundation of the old mercantilist economic system and is a complete reversal of the doctrine of Daniel Raymond. We now realize how Carey was at the same time opposed to both modern protection and to modern liberalism. Carey really goes back of the protectionism of List and Raymond to classical liberalism, and back of liberalism to mercantilism. We cannot therefore find Carey's inspiration in the works of List and Raymond. Whereas Raymond's theory was opposed to that of Smith and Say, Carey tends to return to these writers in order to question the teachings of Malthus and Ricardo. It is not liberalism that he attempts to refute as much as its pessimism. With Carey the reaction of the American economists against the classical school tends to weaken. Yet in the same way that Raymond's reaction against classical economics was different from that of Sismondi's, Carey's reaction goes farther than that of Bastiat. The ultimate explanation of this difference lies again in the contrasts between American and English economic conditions. In the period from Raymond to Carey, these differences were tending to become less striking. If Carey goes beyond Bastiat in reverting to a certain variety of mercantilism, the reason is to be found in the contrast between Continental and English economic conditions, on the one hand; between Continental and American economic conditions, on the other.[1]

Section VI

With Carey the American Reaction Ceases to Be Directed Principally against Adam Smith

Within the English classical school, Carey distinguishes the doctrines of Adam Smith, to which he tends to return, from those of Ricardo and Malthus, to which he is diametrically opposed.

Adam Smith repudiated "trade" by subordinating foreign trade to domestic. More than seventy years have elapsed, said Carey, "since that great man [Adam Smith] denounced the system which looked to compelling the exports of raw produce as one productive of infinite injustice; and, certainly, the histories of Jamaica and Virginia, Ireland and India, since his time, would afford him . . . little reason for changing the opinions." The reduction of foreign trade to second rank and the elevation of domestic trade allows agriculture to benefit by that "natural alliance between the plow and the loom, the harrow and the hammer." Carey regarded trade and manufacture as necessary only to the degree that they contribute to the advancement of agriculture. In reality, it is Smith's deep-rooted agrarianism

---

[1] See Raymond, *Thoughts on Political Economy*, Baltimore, 1820; Turner, *The Ricardian Rent Theory in Early American Economics;* Carey, especially, vol. i, chap. viii.

that Carey is delighted to recover. Land, said Carey, does not demand capital but only the return of her gifts. When a great English landlord speaks of spending five or six pounds per acre, that is all very well, but as usual, real grandeur is in inverse proportion to appearance. The great landlord works with a short lever, the small landowner with a long lever. Nature works slowly but surely, and the more man approaches nature, the more nearly right is he!

Carey also admired Smith's social tendencies and shared his criticism of merchants. The great English economist, said the American, having seen that political action designed to make raw materials and labor cheap was the work of dominant classes, warned England to abandon a system which aimed at the slavery of the people and the ultimate weakening of the community. The *Wealth of Nations* considers man as body and soul; human liberty is its ideal. This ideal could be realized, Smith believed, by subordinating foreign commerce to domestic, by subordinating industry to agriculture, by subordinating land to human labor. The work of Smith, said Carey, remains as the great text-book. Malthus and Ricardo rejected the truths of the *Wealth of Nations* and retained only its errors.

Carey alleged that Smith fell into error by reacting too violently against mercantilism. This led him to take a false view of money as well as of capital, and even led him to justify a certain amount of "trade." Making the mistake of following Hume, Smith came to regard money as an instrument whose quantity was a matter of indifference. Great abundance of money, Smith believed a detriment, since it handicapped foreign trade by raising the price of labor and commodities. What Smith failed to see, according to Carey, was that if an abundance of money raises the price of raw materials and of labor, it simultaneously lowers the price of finished goods: the only important matter in foreign commerce. Moreover, the internal effects of an inflow of money are beneficial, while the external are only slightly disadvantageous. Smith has the audacity, said Carey, to tell us that we could return to a state of barter; yet every time that the quantity of money has diminished, social circulation of wealth has almost ceased and there has been a "glut of commodities of every kind."

If, according to Smith, money is the least useful part of national capital, what, asks Carey, is Smith's meaning of capital. It is neither land, nor labor-power, nor the means of production. No doubt, it is the trivial quantity of goods produced and not yet consumed. In a well organized society, however, the nearer the consumer is to the producer, the smaller is the proportion of capital. "The general industry of society," Carey quotes from Smith, "never can exceed what the capital of the society can employ. . . . No regulation of society can increase the quantity of industry in any direction beyond what its capital can maintain . . . and it is by no means certain that this artificial direction is likely to be more advantageous than that into which it would have gone of its own accord." An absolute error, exclaims Carey. The essential difference between Smith and Carey was simply a conflict between the liberal principle and the mercantilist principle, between non-intervention and intervention. Carey commends Smith for approving the Navigation Act, but condemns him severely for accepting *laissez-faire*.

Smith said that nothing is "more absurd than the whole doctrine of the balance of trade." A nation can import more than it exports for half a century; gold and silver which flows in can be immediately exported; the nation's debts may increase; nevertheless, its real wealth, the exchange value of the nation's land and its labor, may increase in a greater proportion during this period. Providing us with the very foundation of his theory, Carey replies: "Were all this asserted of an individual man, it would be regarded in the highest degree absurd; yet it is here asserted of nations, as though the laws which govern communities of thousands and millions of individuals were not the same with those that govern each of the men of whom they are composed." This reduction of national interest to individual interest is a complete reversal of Raymond's doctrine and the very foundation of the old Mercantile System.[1]

Carey enthusiastically adopts the physiocratic and mercantilist survivals in the *Wealth of Nations* in order to reject with horror the germs of liberalism which were to develop into the political economy of Ricardo and Malthus. Here is just another sample of the many contradictory inspirations borrowed from Adam Smith.

SECTION VII

With Carey the American Reaction Is Concentrated against the Classical Economics of Malthus and Ricardo

Since the school of Malthus and Ricardo had neglected the truths of the *Wealth of Nations* and borrowed only its errors, the teachings of this school, in Carey's opinion, were the very antithesis of political economy. Its doctrines were to political economy as "trade" is to "commerce." Carey's criticism, which had previously been abstract, now takes concrete form.

The source of progress is association. The obstacle to association is distance. Unfortunately, modern political

[1] Carey, vol. i, pp. 284, 333, 414, 417, 420; vol. ii, pp. 108, 216, 452, 463; vol. iii, pp. 105, 126, 206. Cf. also Cossa, chap. xiv.

economy, said Carey, does not recognize this simple fact. Rather it finds the index of national prosperity in the list of importations and exportations. The external goal (imperialism) is attained by means of internal centralization. By means of the extreme specialization, England, for example, wishes to become only a factory, wishes indeed to become the "only workshop of the world." With such a theory of specialization Carey had no sympathy. He cites Goethe's words, the more perfect a body, the more dissimilar become its parts. Carey failed to see that this dictum did not necessarily condemn the English economic policy nor confirm the American. From the English nineteenth-century point of view, international specialization made England only a part of a world body. Carey, on the other hand, whose nation was a continent and nearly a world by itself, saw the nation as the chief end.

Carey levied other criticisms against the English policy. It was not content, he alleged, with separating the producer from the consumer by creating a host of intermediaries, but more particularly, it set about to separate the industrial producers from the agricultural. As a result, the agricultural producer was being sacrificed to the industrial. In the time of Smith, said Carey, there were 200,000 English landowners, while now (1858) there are 34,000. The ruin of agriculture carries with it the ruin of industry. Carey thought it curious that modern political economy had neglected the fact that man is a pure borrower from land and that when he fails to pay his debts, land acts as any other creditor does: by expelling him from her property. England, he said, ends by expelling the people themselves; it is only necessary to consider the number of her emigrants! England's policy favors foreign trade at the expense of domestic by sacrificing agriculture to industry. Moreover, in order to separate producers from consumers, agricultural producers are separated from industrial producers. Such an economic policy, said Carey, has a triple consequence: first, a decrease in the price of services; secondly, a rise in the price of finished products and intermediate goods; finally, and most serious, a fall in the price of labor and a rise in the price of land. These consequences, it will be noted, are just the reverse of Carey's ideal price changes.

The liberal system, Carey tells us, is a struggle for "cheapening labor and raw materials—being precisely the objects sought to be accomplished by the Mercantile System whose error was so well exposed in the *Wealth of Nations.*" Liberalism signifies less economic change than political change. Liberalism, said Carey, is only continued mercantilism, except that political considerations become economic, and national considerations become individual. Economic individualism breaks down the unity of nationalism and transforms the nation from end to means.

Carey's system is opposed to both liberalism and mercantilism; to liberalism because his own system seeks to re-establish national political individuality (the nation as an end) ; to mercantilism because it rejects any means which are designed to subordinate domestic trade to foreign. Carey's mercantilism is therefore a variety of decadent mercantilism, modified by the agrarianism of Cantillon. All the vices of the English economic organization, Carey regarded as the result of the separation of agricultural from industrial producers, and the separation of producers from consumers. While the raw materials for making cloth depreciate in price, the difficulty of obtaining cloth grows greater. Only a small portion of the price paid by the consumer is transmitted to the producer. Yet the English political theory had promised that after the repeal of the corn laws there would be two employers for every laborer, that wages would rise, that money would be abundant, and that wheat would·be cheap. Actually, said Carey, the contrary effect was produced. The rural population has withdrawn from the fields; there are two employees for every employer, and a dozen shop-keepers for every buyer. Whereas Adam Smith's system, said Carey, sought to create competition for the purchase of labor, the Malthusian-Ricardian system creates competition among laborers for the sale of labor. As a result wages constantly fall.

The English policy, said Carey, raises the price of finished goods relative to the price of services, which tend to fall. Worse than that, within the category of services, the price of intermediate goods tends to rise. In other words, the price of capital rises relative to the prices of land and of labor, which tend to fall. Day by day, the accumulations of the past acquire more power over present labor. Meantime the existence of centralized financial organizations compels small savers to invest chiefly in government securities. The English writers, especially John Stuart Mill, have looked upon saving as the chief source of capital. Carey alleged that it is poor countries, like Ireland and Spain, which save the most. Capital, in reality, said Carey, is a saving of labor resulting from association, which is based upon division of tasks. Hence this particular error of the English writers, said Carey, is an outgrowth from their fundamental error: the belief that wealth must be a material substance. The worst result of the English policy that Carey discerned was not that the price of capital rises in relation to that of labor, but that the price of land does likewise. Here, said Carey, we reach the heart of Malthusian-Ricardian economics; here we find the "inverted pyramid." Laborers' incomes diminish, while the number of men and their needs increase.

The whole English economic theory, whether it is defended by Malthus, Ricardo, McCulloch, or even Mill, according to Carey, is from the beginning a "system of discords." Its advocates are in disagreement with one another as well as with the facts. It tends to create war between individuals and between nations. "Professing an admiration for freedom of commerce, he [Ricardo] teaches that a monopoly of the land is in accordance with a great law of nature. Believing in freedom of action, he teaches that if men and women *will* unite in marriage . . . starvation is to be their probable reward. Thoroughly admiring sound morality, he enforces the advantages of celibacy. . . . Professing a desire for free trade in corn, he teaches the landlord that his interests will be injuriously affected by it. . . . Desiring that the rights of property may be respected, he instructs the laborer that the interests of the landowner are to be promoted by every measure tending to produce a scarcity of food. . . . His [Ricardo's] book is the true manual of the demagogue." Is it possible, asks Carey, that the Creator has been inconsistent? Why should he have said "increase and multiply"? He could not have wished for such disorder; no, "the great Architect of the Universe was no blunderer, such as modern political economy would make him. All wise, he was not required to institute different sets of laws for the government of the same matter. All just, he was incapable of instituting any that could be adduced in justification of tyranny and oppression. All merciful, he could make none that would afford a warrant for want of mercy among men toward their fellow-men."

Having thus characterized political economy in a sentence which certainly seems to savor of the "theological stage" of reasoning, Carey ingenuously exclaims, "Is it not clear from this, that social science as taught by Ricardo and his successors, is only in that stage which is designated by M. Comte as the metaphysical one? Could it be otherwise with a system which takes no note of the qualities by which man is distinguished from the beasts of the field?"

According to Carey, this discordant system has its origin in the immorality of a deep-rooted materialism. By forestalling association, the liberal system at the same time prevents the development of the latent faculties of man, reducing him to the condition of the "brute beast." It does not take cognizance of man's distinctive qualities, and remembers only those which he has in common with a wolf or a horse; it recognizes only "the human animal." From this proceeds the immorality of the extolled social relations. One English author could therefore write, "If men will marry, . . . it is for them to take their chance—and that if we stand between the error and its consequences, we stand between the evil and its cure—if we intercept the penalty, we perpetuate the sin." Carey was indignant with a theory which made marriage a social fault. "No theory has ever been published," he wrote, "so calculated to annihilate confidence in the wisdom and beneficence of the Creator." Carey therefore sets about to refute the pessimistic classical economics. Malthus, he said, finds the cause of slavery as "the natural result of a divine, and therefore inevitable, law." The superior classes, being relieved of all responsibility for poverty and misery, can therefore close both their purses and their hearts. As it is taught by Malthus and Ricardo, said Carey, political economy has been well named "a philosophy of despair resting upon an arithmetic of ruin."[1]

Fortunately it is an absolute error, based upon a per-

[1] It would be interesting to compare Carey with the Christian economics which Villeneuve-Bargemont, in 1834, opposed to English economics. Among the advocates of Christian economics were Sismondi, Droz, Morogues, and Saint-Chamans. In his method of presenting the social problem, Villeneuve-Bargemont is similar to Henry George.

verted notion of matter, a relative notion which could only find expression in England. The so-called laws of rent and population, said Carey, are not natural laws, as their authors allege, but the natural consequence of an artificial political economy. To prove this, Carey presents his well-known refutation of the Ricardian theory of rent.

The Ricardian explanation of rent, said Carey, is unsound for two reasons. In the first place, it supposes an historical order of cultivation which is contrary to facts. In taking up land, farmers do not go from rich soils to poor soils, but from poor soils to rich, in the same way that artisans abandon a mediocre tool for a better tool, as primitive man discarded the stone ax for one of iron. Carey then illustrates his theory of the migration of cultivation from poor soils to rich by a multitude of examples drawn from all periods and places. Secondly, in addition to the realistic objection, he also offers a logical objection to the Ricardian hypothesis. To admit the correctness of the English views, said Carey, would be to admit that while the clay, in which the farmer guides his plow, is subject to certain laws, it becomes the object of different laws after having passed through the hands of the potter and having been converted into porcelain.

The Malthusian theory of population, said Carey, is equally incorrect, and this also for two reasons. In the first place, the reproductive function exists in inverse proportion to intellectual development. This is the theory of the balance between nervous and sensual centers. An African ant, for example lays 80,000 eggs. But as the animal order advances, the reproductive capacity diminishes. In the second place, this argument from the positive order is paralleled by a purely logical objection to the Malthusian hypothesis. The Creator, said Carey, would not have established one law by virtue of which matter was required to take its most advanced form, that of man, in a more rapid proportion than it was required to take its lowest form: that of potatoes and beets, of turnips and oysters, necessary for human subsistence. Such is the strongly articulated reasoning of Carey! Rent, due to an increase of population, is compensated by a diminution of rent due to natural factors, to the exact degree that the increase of population leads to a passage of cultivation from poor soils to rich. Carey's doctrine is thus a complete reversal of the classical theory of Malthus and Ricardo. The increase of population does not subordinate man to land; it subordinates land to man! The unity of all matter compels the increase of inferior biological forms to be in proportion to the increase of the superior forms. Moreover, in this process, the increase of superior forms, instead of depending upon the increase of inferior forms, governs the increase of inferior biological forms and compels this increase to its proportionate amounts. At the same time that the historical order of cultivation goes from less to more, the biological order of population goes from more to less.[1]

This final harmony is the very solution of the first problem which was presented. Because the increase of the value of land is only relative and is in no way contradicted by the constant diminution of rent, and because the one factor, in relation to which all others are adjusted, is human labor, only one more problem remains. Since value is always defined as the "power of nature over man," in what sense can one speak of the value of human labor and of the value of man?[2]

[1] Carey, vol. i, pp. 86, 138, 139, 231, 421, 433, 438, 443; vol. ii, pp. 36, 72, 326, 334; vol. iii, pp. 60, 105, 154, 159, 160, 166, 167.
[2] The proof that Carey's criticism is significant, in its general aspects, is that it reappears today in the best recent study of English economic conditions. Cf. Siegfried, A., *L'Angleterre d'Aujourd'hui*, Paris, 1924, especially p. 188. Siegfried's phrase is unconsciously a repetition of Carey: "The whole thing is to

SECTION VIII

*The First Inspiration of H. C. Carey: The American
Political Regime*

If English political conditions help to explain the classical political economy of Malthus and Ricardo, do not
American political conditions help to explain the political
economy of Carey? In his fashion, Carey sketches the
economic history of the United States during the first half
of the nineteenth century. In tracing this history, he alleges
that American commercial policy has followed the British
model, whereas it should have been quite different.

Since the cause of the American Revolution, said Carey,
was the need for freedom from the "colonial system" which
exhausted Ireland and India one would have supposed that
the new nation would have taken the necessary measures to
bring producer and consumer nearer together. Indeed, the
first tendencies of the government were of this kind, as
revealed in Hamilton's *Report on Manufactures.* Industry developed as a result of the cessation of international
trade during the War of 1812. With the return of peace,
however, except for the cotton industry, manufactures were
abandoned to their fate; machinery was unused, entrepreneurs were ruined and workers were reduced to idleness.
An enormous capital was lost to the nation. Land sold for
one-third or even one-fourth of its former value. "Trade"
took the place of "commerce." This universal distress was
remedied by the semi-protective tariff of 1824, and by the

know if the future distribution of industrial production in the world
will continue to support, by a paradoxical division of labor, the
existence within the United Kingdom of a colossal factory and a
market for merchandise without compare."

On the other hand, if we turn from its application to the principle
itself, we find Edwin Cannan taking a stand against pessimistic
Malthusian-Ricardian economics, much in the spirit of Carey. Cf.
Cannan, Edwin, *Wealth,* London, 1923, second edition, chap. iv.

highly protective tariff of 1828, which for the first time instituted the policy of Colbert in the American Union. The protests of the cotton growing states soon led, however, to the Compromise Tariff of 1833, which provided for the gradual termination of protection and was so arranged that by 1842 protection would have completely disappeared. The ruin of commerce, resulting from the lowered duties led to a brief readoption of protection, although this was again largely removed in 1846. "In brief," said Carey, "it may now be stated that the expediency of protection has been recognized in every tariff since the formation of the Federal Constitution in 1789, and that it has more or less existed at every hour except for a few weeks in 1842, but that it has, on only two occasions, been made adequate to the accomplishment of the object for which it is intended, that of raising the prices of raw products . . . and reducing those of manufactured ones. In both those cases, 1828 to 1833 and 1842 to 1846, the laws were repealed almost at the moment when they had fairly begun to become operative."

The inadequacy of protection gave rise to the supremacy of "trade" with its inevitable consequences. Carey dwells upon the formation of association which he observed in the very life of rising cities in the United States. But how does it happen, he asks, that instead of developing association in the East, where resources are still unlimited, people prefer to remove themselves from markets and ceaselessly bury themselves in the western frontier? Is it not because of the spirit of "trade"? Is it not because an agrarian economy has been suffocated by a legal cloak? At the same time that landed property was strengthened, American commercial policy, by reducing the price of wheat in the whole world, reduced the power to buy cloth. The stoppage of the importation of American wheat into

Europe, said Carey, would be a fortunate measure which would compel Europe to turn to agriculture. Not content to follow England, in economic mistakes, Carey alleged that the United States had sometimes even led the way. The monetary restrictions of Robert Peel, for example, were designed to imitate the absurd attitude of the American government, based upon a belief in the quantity theory of money.

The American policy, Carey further alleged, lacked the constancy of the English policy. Instability was rather its characteristic; a perpetual balancing of good and bad policy. Protection ended in 1818, bequeathing to free trade general prosperity, an excess of exports, a large revenue, a smaller public debt. Free trade ended in 1824, bequeathing to protection general impoverishment, an excess of imports, a diminished revenue and an increased public debt. This wavering was repeated in 1834–35 when protection again disappeared before free trade, in 1842 when free trade gave way to protection, and finally, in 1847, when free trade superseded protection.

This instability, said Carey, has various causes. In transportation policy, the United States has constantly followed Cromwell and Colbert in the path of wise protection. In the realm of finance, decentralization has been accomplished. Just the reverse of the centralization of London or Paris, the multiplication of small banks in the United States assures the localization of capital. Yet in spite of this excellent regime, the last half-century witnessed two suspensions by all the banks of the country. Financial decentralization is therefore neutralized by the bad effects of general economic centralization. Finally, this instability of policy is due to the fact that economic centralization coexists with political decentralization. Like France, America is a "country of contrasts," but whereas in France, a centralized political system is combined with a decentralized economic system, in America the situation is exactly reversed.[1]

We must now recognize that there was, in addition to the American political situation, a second inspiration for Carey's work: the French economic regime.

SECTION IX

The Second Inspiration of H. C. Carey: The French Economic Regime

Carey's systematic mind delighted in the above-mentioned contrasts. Whereas in England, the economics of Malthus and Ricardo was only an interpretation of English trade, in France, as in the United States, there was disagreement between theory and practice. But whereas the French practice, said Carey, is that of "commerce," the American practice is that of "trade"; and whereas the French theory is that of "trade," the American theory is that of "commerce." In France, there is disagreement as a result of doctrine, in the United States as a result of facts. All this, however, is true only in a general sense. In England, the prevailing economic doctrine is only the theory of English trade qualified by the Smithian contribution. In the United States the facts are in disagreement with the theory of "commerce." In France the theory of "trade" is in disagreement with the policy of commerce.

The French economic organization, said Carey, is admirable. Indeed there are two economic systems before the world. The object of one is realized by increasing competi-

---

[1] Carey, vol. ii, pp. 176, 177, 178, 182, 186, 187, 190, 206, 217, 272, 419, 434, 438; vol. iii, p. 207. With the reservations necessary to Carey's economic history of the United States, compare Taussig, F. W., *Tariff History of the United States,* 6th edition, 1907, pp. 120 ff.

tion for the sale of raw materials; the other seeks to increase competition in the purchase of raw materials. The first is the English system; the second is that of France; the system of Colbert, "the most distinguished of all the sons of France." Carey is enraptured with French protectionism. He maintained that the result of Napoleon's Continental Blockade was "to form an era in the history of German, as well as in that of French, industry; though J. B. Say, the most celebrated disciple of Adam Smith, has stigmatized it as a calamity." With the decay of rural England, Carey delights to contrast the prosperity of French agriculture. From 1760 to 1840, said Carey, the production of cereals in France has increased in greater proportion than the increase in population. The only blemish on the French policy, in his estimation, was the existence of financial centralization. Yet, in spite of this blemish, it is only by following the policy of France that most European nations can protect themselves against the pre-eminence of "trade," which is designed to make England "the only workshop of the world."

If the French doctrine, said Carey, does not absolutely agree with this admirable economic system, it at least has the merit of rejecting the economics of Malthus and Ricardo. Dunoyer criticized the restriction of wealth to material things. Carey's position, midway between Dunoyer and Say, corresponds to reality. De Fontenay had clearly shown that capital is a saving of labor. Against the very disciples of Say, Carey defends the law of markets. He criticizes Blanqui severely for having written that one need no longer "look, as in the days of Adam Smith, exclusively to the acceleration of production; it being required now to govern it—restraining it within wise limits. It is no longer a question of absolute but of relative wealth—humanity requiring that we should cease to sacrifice to the progress

of general opulence, the great masses of the people who cannot profit by it." [1]   Actually economic conditions in America
preserve an environment which was ephemeral in Europe.
Yet, a similar, though brief situation, in France, had led
Say to place great emphasis upon production. It is rather
meaningful to see Carey thus deliberately interposing himself between the French master and his disciples. Finally,
citing de Tocqueville and citing Baudrillart, Carey states
with satisfaction that not only has the Malthusian-
Ricardian theory been generally repudiated by the French
economists, but that Bastiat himself has adopted the grand
harmonious law of distribution.

Whatever the merits of the French theory, it nevertheless does not correspond with the French practice. After
having successively praised Colbert, Hume, and Adam
Smith (who approved of the Navigation Act), Carey added,
"Much more fully than Dr. Smith, did Mr. J. B. Say appreciate the necessity for action on the part of the co-
ordinating power, circumstances, in his opinion, greatly
modifying the proposition generally true, that each and
every individual is capable of judging for himself as to the
most advantageous mode of employing his capital and his
labor. Smith wrote, as M. Say well saw, in a country
whose government has shown itself little disposed to
neglect its interests." Blanqui, Rossi, Moreau de Jonnés,
said Carey, all realized the part of protection. As to
Chevalier, Carey raised the question whether he is anxious
to safeguard free trade. But who would benefit by free
trade? Would it be the French peasant or the American
farmer? What value has this novel interpretation of Say?
It shows, perhaps, that the importance of a doctrine is for
him only relative; it contains also, in spite of the common
prejudice which attributes an absolute liberalism to J. B.

[1] Blanqui, *Histoire d'économique politique,* vol. ii, p. 146.

Say, a good deal of truth. Be that as it may, Carey invokes Say not only to oppose Chevalier, but also to combat the free trade theory of Bastiat. The latter tells his readers, said Carey, that protective tariffs are only another form of communism. This is absolutely false. What renders protection necessary is the need of combining various efforts whereby the productivity of labor can be increased. Protection is necessary, because free trade places fortune and happiness at the mercy of a distant nation. The problem of protection is whether a people should or should not maintain a foreign government in addition to its own government. France supports its own government; Ireland and the United States support those of others. Moreover, Bastiat, according to Carey, illustrates the habitual inconsistency of the modern school. Although he opposes protective duties, he admits fiscal duties. Yet the latter are perpetual, while the former are only temporary.

The French theory, Carey continued, disavows not only French policy but the French economy. Bastiat defends Turkey, Ireland, and India, none of whom can buy gold; and condemns France, Germany, Belgium, all of whom can furnish themselves with gold and silver. Following the English authors, Bastiat regards the quantity of money as a matter of indifference. But he fails to realize the connection between money and commerce. He overlooks the social function of money. In the light of the real harmony of interests which exist in the economic world, it is quite proper for Bastiat to repudiate the saying of Montaigne that "the profit of one is the loss of another." But why does he then proceed to contradict himself and actually adopt Montaigne's dictum in his explanation of money?

If we proceed from money to value, said Carey, here again, on this supreme point, we find Bastiat in error. He ranks intermediaries in the same category with agriculturalists and reproaches socialism for making them parasites. It is true that the intermediary is a creator of value, but he *only* creates value, not wealth. For this reason, men rejoice when they can dispense with the service of the intermediary. Since value is the measure of the power of nature over man, the value of man increases proportionally as the value of commodities declines; conversely whenever the trader adds to the value of commodities, an equal amount is subtracted from the value of man. But in what sense does Carey speak of the value of man?[1]

Section X

The Third Inspiration of H. C. Carey: The Works of J. B. Say, Which Really Provide a Common Origin of Similar Ideas in Carey and Bastiat

How can the differences between Bastiat and Carey be explained if the former, as it is alleged, was only a plagiarist of the latter? The *Economic Harmonies* were published in 1850, at the same time as Carey's *Harmony of Interests*. This was before the publication of the *Principles of Social Science* (1858–59), but after the *Principles of Political Economy* (1837–38–40) and after *The Past, Present and the Future* (1848). How can one explain the differences between the two authors if Bastiat's work is only a copy of Carey's? The Carey-Bastiat controversy is famous. Professor Ferrara reluctantly admitted that "Bastiat published his *Harmonies* taken wholesale as to facts, figures, and philosophy from the works of Carey. The flashes of wit of the great plagiarist quickly become a dead weight in the hands of propagandists who by mishap have taken for a philosophy that which was only

[1] Carey, vol. i, p. 193; vol. ii, pp. 471, 472, 476; vol. iii, pp. 426, 429, 434, 441, 442, 453.

pleasantry. Such is always the fate of scientific protago-
nists. Thus Smith's Wealth of Nations could not be ex-
tensively studied until J. B. Say had methodically re-worked
it; moreover the original was no longer read after the publication of Say's interpretation." But is not this appraisal
of the French economist entirely too severe?

Bastiat admitted that he had read Carey. It is not at
all doubtful that he was influenced by Carey; one need
only compare a few passages to appreciate the bonds which
connect the two writers. Bastiat places in relief the
analogy between the social body and the human body. In
the unity of the social and material world the divine plan
is reflected. No more than Carey, did he believe that this
unity excluded a given ruling order: "As much as intelligence is above all matter, so much is the social world
above that world which Newton admired, for celestial
mechanics obeys laws of which it is not conscious." For
our spiritualist, therefore, every atom of the social world
is endowed with liberty. Like Carey, Bastiat places in
relief the primary rôle of association within the social
world. The only difference is that Bastiat renames it
"solidarity." This natural solidarity is the woof and warp
of his *Harmonies*. This solidarity is natural, not so much
because its end is the individual, but because its means
is free individual effort. The development of association
draws the producer nearer to the consumer. This increasing integration of the economic world reveals a harmony
where Malthus saw only discord.

The pessimistic view of Ricardo is replaced by a different and more exact notion of value. Value is not in-
corporated labor, but saved labor. Progress marks a
constant diminution of value; that is to say, of the cost of
reproduction. How can rent exist when the value of products cannot exceed the expenses of production (in which

gratuitous natural utility does not enter)? Bastiat is content to extend to land the distributive law of capital. Rent
appears to him, in accordance with the old physiocratic
view, derived less from the niggardliness of nature than
from her liberality. Rent was a gain of man over nature,
but a gain of man over nature by means of an investment
of capital. "In short," wrote Bastiat, "an economy of
forces has been realized. To the profit of whom? To the
profit of the two contractual parties. What is the law
governing the partition of this gain over nature? The law
which we have often cited with regard to capital: that as
capital increases, the share of the capitalist or proprietor
increases in absolute value and diminishes in relative value;
while the share of the laborer or the consumer increases in
both absolute and relative value." Full of sympathy for
Malthus, Bastiat only attempts to refute him in part. As
to Ricardo's theory, Bastiat scarcely skims the surface.

In brief, harmony of the social and material world;
within the social world, the primary rôle of association;
the drawing together of producer and consumer; the same
admiration for Dunoyer's theory of "immaterial products";
the same law of value and harmony of distribution—these
are some of the points common to the French and the
American author. Not only did Bastiat have recourse to
Carey, but when this inspiration was lacking, he is inferior
to his usual self or rather to his American guide. This
is clearly revealed by comparing Bastiat's attitude toward
Ricardo-Malthusianism with that of Carey.

Yet if Bastiat was merely a copyist, how shall we explain
the points of contrast which even Carey himself pointed
out between his doctrine and Bastiat's? Perhaps it may
be explained by difference of environment. The divergence
between American and European economic conditions gives
us the key not only to the points of radical difference be-

tween the two authors, but also to the inferiorities as well as the superiorities of Bastiat in his imitation. If the difference in environment will partly liberate Bastiat from the sad rôle that has been ascribed to him, the very coincidence of some enveloping ideas makes it possible to sift out Bastiat's own contribution. For there are some fundamental differences between the political theory, economic theory, and social views of Bastiat as contrasted with Carey.

Bastiat's political theory seems more logical than that of Carey: free competition in the external sphere tends to intensify domestic free competition. "If it is true," wrote Bastiat, "as to me it appears incontestible, that the various nations of the globe will be led by competition to exchange only labor between them at a progressively smaller sacrifice, how blind and absurd are those who repel foreign goods legislatively under the pretext that they are cheap, that they do not have value relative to their total utility, that is to say, precisely because they contain a great portion of gratuitous utility!" And after having eulogized the United States, where free trade reigns, Bastiat added, "I am deceived. There are two active causes of revolution in the United States: slavery and the restrictive regime. Everyone knows that at every moment these two questions imperil public peace and the federal unity." But the very American conditions supported Carey rather than Bastiat. The new protection, "the American system," as Sidney Sherwood pointed out, was altogether different from the old mercantilism. The mercantilist political unit was the nation; the protectionist political unit was a federation, an empire. The real characteristic of the "American system" is therefore that external protection is paralleled with internal free trade. America is a continent within which free trade operates. What a difference as compared with

Europe. Moreover, if one really goes to the bottom of things, perhaps it is Carey rather than Bastiat who better deserves the title of free-trader. Besides, as free trade expands, political unity becomes subordinate to economic unity. Just the reverse of Raymond's protectionism, Carey's system does not make economic unity rest upon political unity at all. Rather, it is political unity which is founded upon economic unity. The political unity so founded is no longer monarchical, but democratic. Henceforth, only that protection is legitimate which aims at the interest of all.

The American milieu explains not only the divergence between the commercial policy advocated by Carey and Bastiat respectively, it likewise allows us to understand the inferiority of Bastiat's whole theory of economics. If Bastiat's refutation of the pessimism of Malthus and Ricardo cannot compare with that of Carey, it is because Carey found his refutation actually living in the marvelous expansion of American economic life. We know how Malthusian-Ricardian economics is bound up with free trade politics and how both emanated naturally from the English milieu. Contrariwise, the American facts could only suggest a protectionist policy and a dynamic economy. In the decade from 1830 to 1840, population increased 32%, and in the next decade 35%. The per capita wealth, in 1860, was more than double that of 1840. From 1830 to 1850, railroad mileage increased from 23 miles to more than 3000. Philadelphia, the native city of Carey, was the principal railroad center. At the same time that the extension of means of communication developed national solidarity, the settlers passed from poor soils to fertile soils, and the very increase of population was the primary source of progress. The isolation of America and her infinite resources, the necessity of avoiding transportation costs from Europe to America, the increasing returns from virgin soils, the commercialization of landed property, the absence of opposition, not only between landlords and tenants but between agricultural and industrial classes, the fact that the value of farms did not exceed the cost of improvements, the constant transformation of villages into large towns, a dispersed and individualistic population, a Yankee versatility and the characteristic ability to be a "jack of all trades," capital, money and labor in high demand—all these facts gave life to Carey's works and opposed him diametrically to Raymond and to Malthus. The English pessimists took a static point of view. Carey, the optimist, animated by idealism and overflowing with the exuberance of young America, took a dynamic point of view. This divergence of view-point shows us that the doctrines are more complementary than antagonistic. Bastiat's reaction against Malthusian-Ricardian pessimism lacks the realism which animates Carey's work.

Where then did Bastiat imbibe his copious optimism? In the social trend of the French milieu. If the differences of environment explain the different political ideas of our two authors, if the qualities peculiar to the American milieu explain the general theoretical inferiority of Bastiat, the qualities peculiar to the French milieu gave birth to the superior social impulses of the French author. In truth, the French social atmosphere which inspired Saint-Simon, Fourier, Proudhon, and many others, was, as it is today, more advanced than the American social atmosphere and also the English, where socialist doctrines were barely separated from political economy. From this French milieu arose the clarity of Bastiat (who classes pessimistic economists and socialists among his enemies). From this came also Bastiat's remarkable analysis of "troc simple, circulaire et composé," that ingenious reduction of social

considerations to individual, splendid points which we cannot stress here. We must content ourselves with showing
that, as contrasted with the English economists, the economic theory of Bastiat is optimistic; that, as contrasted
with the socialists, his socialism (in which the individual
is not only the end but the means) is natural; and finally,
that his optimistic economics and his natural socialism tend
toward a social economy which represents a definite progress over J. B. Say.[1]

Section XI

Proof of a Common Inspiration of Carey and Bastiat

We have seen that the lack of co-incidence between
American and European economic facts and between British and Continental economic facts explains the differences
between Bastiat and Carey. This lack of realistic co-
incidence likewise explains both Bastiat's inferiorities and
his superiorities. Yet in spite of this lack of realistic co-
incidence, there was a co-incidence of ideas between Carey
and Bastiat which made possible Bastiat's own contribution to economic theory. We shall now compare the two
authors with J. B. Say and at the same time raise a final
question. We recall that for Carey, value is the power of
nature over man, that value is measured not by the cost
of production but by the cost of reproduction, not by em-
bodied labor but by saved labor. When Carey speaks of
augmenting the value of man, however, he forgets that he
has defined value as the "power of nature over man."

[1] See: Bastiat, *Oeuvres Completes,* vol. vi; also *Harmonies
Économiques,* 3d. Edition, Paris, 1854, pp. 9, 35, 37, 39, 45, 47, 48,
63, 69, 70, 73, 74, 75, 76, 77, 87, 89, 90, 91, 97, 99, 101, 103, 104, 106,
122, 123, 126, 128, 129, 134, 135, 136, 138, 142, 143, 147, 153, 154,
157, 162, 177, 186, 197, 223, 247, 248, 259, 328, 356, 361, 378, 407,
435, 448, 450, 482, 485, 503, 534; cf. also Gide and Rist, part iii,
chap. i.

This contradiction, although more formal than real, must have originated from the influence of a badly assimilated doctrine of J. B. Say.

Numerous details prove what Carey owed to Say. Does not Carey's substitution of "social science" for "political economy" suggest Say's preference for "l'économie sociale"? Is it not in Say that Carey found the germ of his distinction between "changes of place," "changes of form," and "vital changes in the form of matter" unless he got it from Destutt de Tracy?[1] Other similarities between Say and Carey may be found in the defense of political decentralization, the subordination of foreign trade to domestic, the admission of immaterial products, and the conception of capital arising less from saving than from production. If the geographical drawing together of producer and consumer (which Carey would effect by the suppression of "trade") recalls the Physiocrats, the economic *rapprochement* which ends with the pre-eminence of the consumer recalls Say.

It must be remembered, in surveying these details, that Carey had two sets of fundamental ideas: political and economic. We have seen that for the American economist "real freedom of trade" was only the application of Say's law of markets. In reality, Carey's doctrine was the second inference which Say drew from his law: "A city surrounded by a rich countryside is provided with numerous and rich buyers; and, in the neighborhood of an opulent city, the products of the country have much higher value. It is by a futile distinction that one classifies na-

[1] *A Treatise on Political Economy,* to which is prefixed a supplement to a preceding work on the understanding or Elements of Idealogy, with an analytical table and an introduction on the faculty of the will, by the Count de Stutt de Tracy, member of the Senate and Institute of France and of the American Philosophical Society; translated from the unpublished French original. Georgetown, 1817. See, p. 19.

tions as agricultural, manufacturing, or commercial. If a nation succeeds in agriculture, this is the reason why its manufactures and its commerce prosper; if its manufacturing and its commerce are flourishing, its agriculture will improve. A nation, in relation to a neighboring nation, is in the same status as one province is to another, as a city is to the country; each is interested in seeing the other prosper; since its own prosperity is thereby increased. Quite rightly, therefore, have the United States always sought to provide industry for the tribal savages with whom they are surrounded; they have wished these savages to have something to give in exchange, because one can gain nothing from people who have nothing to give in exchange. It is precious for humanity that one nation among others conducts itself in every circumstance in accordance with the liberal principles. It will demonstrate by the brilliant results that it will obtain that the vain systems, the baneful theories of other nations are really founded upon exclusive and jealous maxims of the old states of Europe which have brazenly been dignified with the name of practical truths, unfortunately put into practice. The American Union will have the glory of proving by experience that the highest political action is in accord with moderation and humanity." Whatever illusions Say may have entertained, however inferior to Sismondi (that perspicacious reformer) [1] his insight may have been, one can understand how Carey was able to find in Say the germ of a theory of protection which would guard agriculture against the inroads of industry. One understands it even more clearly, for, although the author of the *Traité d'économie politique* may have stigmatized the Continental blockade, the old manufacturer of Auchy remembered with satisfac-

[1] Cf. Sismondi, *Nouveaux Principes*, vol. i, pp. 296, 325, 340, 426, 431; vol. ii, pp. 8, 9, 30, 31, 108, 111, 224, 230.

tion the prosperity of the imperial economic regime; an economic regime whose importance cannot be exaggerated, as it anticipated the American system and gave Continental Europe momentary free trade behind a customs barrier.

Still it is less Carey's political theory than Carey's very economic theory which reminds one of J. B. Say. For Say's doctrine is entirely contained in the question which he liked to ask: "If the value of the products which a nation possesses constitutes the wealth of that nation, how can this nation become richer when its products fall in price?" The answer is simple. In the first place, for Say, value is a ratio of exchange (the value of a thing being in direct proportion to the quantity of other things which it commands in exchange) and, in the second place, beyond simple exchange is to be found the fundamental exchange of production (an exchange not of goods for goods, but products for services). These premises being assumed, even though the value of products does constitute the wealth of a nation, yet this nation becomes richer when products decrease in price. All values being relative, the decrease in the value of products means conversely a rise in the value of services. When this principle, so fundamental in Carey's reasoning, is found in J. B. Say, there seems to be little doubt but that Carey borrowed from Say not only the idea that wealth increases in proportion to the decrease in the value of products, but also the idea that wealth increases in proportion to the rise in the value of man. Because Carey failed to bind together this twofold price interaction by means of an adequate theory of value (the idea of exchange value), his theory, in consequence, is disjointed.

Like Carey, Bastiat also found the germs of his theory of value in J. B. Say. For Bastiat, as well as his American contemporary, value is measured by the cost of reproduction: by the amount of saved labor. Bastiat, however, introduces a new notion of service which contrasts him both with Carey and with Say. The word "service" in Say's doctrine had a meaning more technical than social. According to Bastiat, the substance of "service," and consequently of value, was what he calls "onerous utility" as opposed to "gratuitous utility." "Value," said he, "is proportional to the service rendered and not at all to the absolute utility of the thing, because this utility can be, to a very large extent, the result of a gratuitous action of nature." The utility of a material product is in its matter, but its value in its service. "Gratuitous utility" tends cumulatively to become common; "onerous utility," the substance of value and alone appropriable, tends constantly to be reduced. The weapon which Say gave to the socialists was his theory that nature not only created utility but value itself. "One might have believed," said Bastiat of Say, "that he had fulfilled his mission as an economist as well by extending the value of products to service as in bringing back value from service to products had not socialist propaganda, based upon his very deductions, arisen to reveal the insufficiency and the dangers of his principle. Having asked myself this question: since certain products have value and since certain services have value, then since value, identical with itself, can have only one origin, one *raison d'être*, one identical explanation, is this origin, this explanation, in the product or in the service? I say boldly that the question does not appear doubtful for an instant for the incontrovertible reason which is this: every product which has value implies a service, whereas every service does not necessarily suppose the existence of a product. By this, I affirm that the theory which defines wealth in terms of value is only the glorification of obstacles; here is the syllogism: wealth is proportional to value, value to efforts, efforts to obstacles; therefore, wealth is proportional to obstacles." Hence Bastiat reproaches Say for confusing utility and value, on the one hand; value and wealth, on the other. All of which indicates that Bastiat did not grasp, any more than Carey did, the importance of Say's exchange of production (which was Say's outline of economic equilibrium). Bastiat failed to recognize that in Say's theory, although "onerous utility" was the essence of the value of products, "gratuitous utility" was the essence of the value of human services, and consequently, of wealth. Both Carey and Bastiat, without completely understanding their common inspirer, borrowed from him the essential idea of this automatic way in which progress could be abbreviated. But Bastiat borrowed more than Carey, and for this reason he surpasses Carey. Service signifies not only effort but social effort. There is no value in a state of nature. Service is effort on the part of a person other than the person who experiences the want. Value is therefore a ratio, a ratio between two exchanged services. For this reason, "exchange does more than state and measure values, it creates their existence. In isolation, with what can effort be compared? With need? With satisfaction? In the social state, the effort of one man is compared with the effort of another man, two phenomena of the same nature, and consequently, commensurable."

Thus it is that the realistic non-co-incidence of material milieus permits us partially to release Bastiat from the charge of plagiarism, which has been made against him. Conversely, the very co-incidence of the intellectual milieu, an identical doctrinal atmosphere, makes it possible to sift out Bastiat's own contribution.[1]

[1] Cf. Say. *Traité,* especially, pp. 57, 140, 141, 212; *Cours* (1844), especially p. 58, and chapters ix and xv.

Conclusion

To distinguish Bastiat's own contribution is, at the same stroke, to determine that of Carey. We have seen that the political theory of the American economist is concerned with an harmonious juxtaposition of agricultural production and a domestic economic policy, on the one hand; and with industrial production and an external economic policy, on the other. The relation between these should be the subordination of the external industrial policy to the domestic agricultural policy; that is, of politics to economics. But from the pre-eminence of agriculture over industry, in Carey's theory, we cannot conclude that it presumes a pre-eminence of land, as a factor of production, over labor. Going from the source of value to value itself, we have seen that association, based upon the division of labor (which is strengthened by mechanical and technical progress) not only links production and consumption geographically, but in a time-period also. The prices of finished and of intermediate goods recede before the price of services, and the price of land decreases as compared with the price of labor.

After having traced this pure theory, an attempt was next made to recreate realistically the facts and circumstances which inspired it. Instead of following Daniel Raymond, Carey actually returned to the teachings of Smith and Say (whom Raymond especially opposed and criticized) in order to oppose himself to the pessimistic classical economics of Malthus and Ricardo. With both Carey and Bastiat, it was not so much liberalism to which they were opposed as the pessimism of liberalism. Nevertheless, Carey's reaction against English economic thought was different from that of Sismondi and from that of Bastiat. As to the resemblances between the works of

Carey and Bastiat, these are largely explicable by the lack of co-incidence in the material environment of the two authors combined with a co-incidence of their respective intellectual environments. The fact that Carey and Bastiat were both inspired by the same author, J. B. Say, explains these resemblances better than the legend of plagiarism. Carey's work does not suffer if light is thrown on its origins. Rather, Carey takes a new place in the history of French economic doctrines. From this point of view, it was the developed doctrine of J. B. Say that Bastiat refound in Carey.[1]

[1] One cannot exaggerate the rôle of J. B. Say in the United States. Say's *Treatise* was the foremost American text book until 1880, that is, until the renaissance of American economic thought under the influence of the German Historical School, and until the re-adoption of contact with English classical economics and hedonism. Since Arthur Perry (1830–1905) was only a disciple of Bastiat, it is necessary to study the various members of Carey's school in order to understand the remarkable imprint of Say's doctrine. In 1832, there appeared in Philadelphia: *A Treatise of Political Economy on the Production, Distribution and Consumption of Wealth, by J. B. Say; translated from the fourth edition of the French by C. R. Princep, M. A. with notes by the translator, Fifth American Edition containing a translation of the introduction and additional notes by Clement C. Biddle, Member of the American Philosophical Society.* These notes applied Say's theory with an inflexible logic. But many more than five editions were published. The two first editions, of 1821 and 1824 (published in Boston) were followed by those of 1827, 1830, 1832, 1834, 1836, 1841, 1845, 1848, 1852, 1854, 1857, 1859 (Philadelphia); in a quarter of a century, more than fourteen editions, twice as many American as French editions. Four years before the first American edition of Say's Treatise and at the same time that Destutt de Tracy's work, through Jefferson's efforts, was published at Georgetown, *The Catechism of Political Economy,* (translated by Richter in London in 1816) was published in the United States (1817). It was edited and published by H. C. Carey and his father. At the age of 24, therefore, Carey was acquainted with the theory of the French economist. The proof is in the yellow pages of the *Catechism of Political Economy, or Familiar Conversations on the Manner in which Wealth is Produced, Distributed, and Consumed in Society, by J. B. Say, Professor of Political Economy in the Athénée Royal of Paris, Knight of St. Wolodomir of Russia, Member of the Societies of Zurich, Bologna,* etc., *and author of a Treatise of Political Economy, Translated from the French by John Richter, Philadelphia. Printed and Published by M. Carey, and Son. No. 126 Chestnut Street, May 17, 1817.*

CHAPTER III

THE SOCIAL ECONOMICS OF HENRY GEORGE

SECTION I

Life, General Ideas, and Method of Henry George

Henry George was born in Philadelphia on September 2, 1839.[1] After a brief education, he embarked as a sailor for Australia and India. On his return to the United States, he learned the printing trade. He was soon attracted by the allurement of the West, and went by sea to California. Unfortunately his hope of making a fortune in the newly-discovered gold fields was not realized. Frequently penniless and often head over heels in debt, George floated about from one newspaper to another. Although he was a Protestant, he married a Catholic, and this first step toward Catholicism was not without importance. While his family was always in the throes of misery, Henry George, the pure Jeffersonian democrat, dabbled in San Francisco politics. From a printer he became a newspaper editor, later a petty public officer: inspector of gas meters. In 1877, as a result of some leisure time, he began *Progress and Poverty,* which was published, not without difficulty, in 1879, in New York. This famous work is an expression of George's youthful dreams of gold, his ardent desire for fortune, and of his defeat, a defeat largely explicable by his fundamental honesty and his respect for truth. Moreover, there is manifest in *Progress and Poverty* the intense

[1] See George, Henry, *Progress and Poverty* New York, 1924; *The Life of Henry George, by his son Henry George, Jr.,* New York, 1900; cf. also Speek, Peter Alexander, *The Single Tax and the Labor Movement,* Madison, Wisconsin, 1917.

allurement of the West, most intense at the time when George wrote, because the American frontier was on the verge of disappearance. What part, in George's work, did the exuberant individualism of the frontier really play? We shall see.

An industrial revolution had followed the close of the Civil War. As early as 1860, the network of railroads in the United States exceeded the mileage of all the European railroads and Henry George was himself able to travel from New York to San Francisco over the Central Pacific which had been built during the war. The expansion of means of communication had increased the value of domestic commerce from three billions in 1860 to twenty billions in 1900 (which equaled the foreign commerce of all the nations of the world). American foreign trade during the second half of the nineteenth century, increased tenfold in spite of the constant increase of the tariff. After 1876, American exports exceeded imports. Moreover, a profound change was taking place in the character of exports: manufactured goods were displacing agricultural. The United States, the leading agricultural nation of the world, was also to become the leading industrial nation.

This double economic supremacy of the United States, partially explained by the contributions of immigrant labor, also explains how this flood of immigrants could be absorbed. Yet, despite this great inflowing human tide, the number of immigrants during the second half of the century did not equal the population of the United States during the first half. Hence, although land became the "short factor" as a consequence of population growth, it was not labor which was the "long factor." Although, by 1882, all free land had been taken up, and although there was no longer a frontier, the industrial revolution influenced agriculture to such an extent that its limits, at one time apparently reached, are still being extended. From 1860 to 1880, the production of wheat increased twice as fast as population. Over the longer period from 1850 to 1900 there was an harmonious balance between population and agricultural production; each increased threefold. The significant point is that although labor was still the short factor, this is explained by the American industrial revolution, by the progressive substitution of capital for land as the long factor. From 1850 to 1900, the value of industrial products increased twelvefold. The crises of 1873 and 1893 scarcely interrupted this marvelous economic progress.[1]

The last half of the nineteenth century was a brief triumph of Carey's "real freedom of trade," although domestic commerce was already tending to become subordinated to foreign trade, and although agriculture was tending to become subordinated to industry. The equilibrium between industry and agriculture was disturbed. Foreign imperialism and political corruption was placing domestic economy at the service of a plutocracy. Around 1850, Carey forecast the economic trend of his country up to the end of the century. By 1880, he would probably, like George, have sought to discern the merits of the future beyond the defects of the present. The purest product of Carey's work is, consequently, found less in American facts than in Henry George, who cherished Carey's ideal, in spite of the fact that this ideal had been perverted by the trend of American economic history.

Progress and Poverty, the psychological product of Henry George's failure as a young man, was the success of his life. In but a little while George, the recluse, was well-

[1] Cf. Bogart, *Economic History of the United States;* Clark, Victor, *History of Manufactures;* Faulkner, H. U., *American Economic History.*

known and actively engaged in propagating his ideas. He became passionately interested in the Irish movement; he went to Ireland on several occasions to foment interest in land nationalization and revolution. The economic trend in the United States provided him with an even larger area of reform and re-kindled the enthusiasm which the Irish situation had illicited. Powerfully backed by Mac-Glynn, a priest who resembles Lamennais in his struggle against the Catholic hierarchy, George became a candidate for mayor of New York, in 1886. He was defeated by a very small margin. This partial success is explained by the support which he received from a certain group of Catholic voters, from convinced "single taxers" and from a heterogenous third group of voters. This last group was a curious mixture. It comprised: 1. members of the Central Labor Union of New York, which had been founded in 1881 and which, by 1883, included 70,000 adherents; 2. the Knights of Labor, an order founded in Philadelphia, in 1869, and which, in 1886, had some 50,000 members; 3. "Greenbackers," a complex group of voters whose extreme individualism was opposed to the pure Marxism of a fourth and last group; namely, 4. the Socialists, mostly Germans of recent immigration. Such a curious coalition could not long hold together, and, as a consequence, the first political success of Henry George was not repeated. In the dissolution of this coalition, one of the most important factors was the conflict between the "single taxers" (who followed George's theory and regarded land rent as the source of all social evil) and the Marxians (for whom the fundamental opposition was between capital and labor). Beyond the transitional form of economic organization, Henry George, the Anglo-Saxon socialist, saw a vision of a more distant, but more desirable, social and economic structure. Karl Marx and Friedrick Engels considered him a "bourgeois" and a reactionary. George was not their type of a reformer; he agreed more nearly with Carlyle, Ruskin, and Alfred Russell Wallace. In reality, George was a mystic with his hand on the Bible and with a belief that he was invested with a divine mission. And no one has given Henry George sweeter praise than that profound individualistic agrarian, Leo Tolstoy.

From the American economists, from his compatriots, however, George received no praise. Their criticisms were pitiless, especially because the fright which George's writings and activity momentarily created had been great. Haney has written that *"Progress and Poverty . . .* aroused an interest and provoked such debate that we of a later generation still hear its echoes while hardly realizing its intensity." The first attitude of the economists was to ignore George. When George refused to submit to the disdain of silence, his method and his doctrine was passed through a sieve of severe criticism. Among the outstanding critics of George was Francis A. Walker, who, in 1877, two years before the publication of *Progress and Poverty,* had also attacked the wages-fund doctrine and who, following Say, had distinguished profits from interest in order to resolve profits into rent. There were also Alfred Marshall, R. T. Ely, E. R. A. Seligman, F. W. Taussig, and W. A. Scott, all of whom turned their attention to refuting the theories of George. Yet how important were all these criticisms, if J. B. Clark admitted that he was indebted to the author of *Progress and Poverty?*

Although self-taught, George rapidly acquired a knowledge of economic literature. Before the publication of *Progress and Poverty,* he professed to have read only Herbert Spencer's *Social Statics* which was, in a sense, to George what Comte's writings were to Carey. In his later works, however, George's references to economic literature are abundant. He refers to Hobbes, Guizot, Say, Malthus, Ricardo, Fawcet, Torrens, McCulloch, Rae, Senior, J. S. Mill, Bowen, Jevons, MacLeod, de Laveleye, Walker, Clark, Michelet, Laughlin, Ruskin, Böhm-Bawerk, Marshall, and others.

In one of his sketches, George indicates clearly his meaning of political economy and the general outlines of his conception of the science. While political economy should furnish a powerful aid to ethics, it does not pronounce itself in favor of justice and opposed to injustice. Howsoever it may be connected with politics, its direct object is only those natural laws which govern the production and the distribution of wealth. If we wish to speak of political economy both as a science and an art, it is the "noble art" which wishes to realize the good of all the members of the economic community; it is nothing short of socialism. This social utilitarianism is, however, only the means of attaining complete individual naturalism. We recognize, therefore, the abyss which separates George's socialism from Marxian socialism. The latter, said George, takes no account of natural laws and is an art as artificial as politics. It has no system of individual rights to limit those of the state.[1]

In George's opinion, both the Historical School and the Neo-classical school suffer from the same defect, although in different degree. Today, he said, one no longer speaks of "political economy," but of "economics" which teaches that there are no external natural laws and which in reply to the question of the superiority of protection or free trade, alleges that this depends upon time and place. George ridicules the incomprehensible works of Marshall and the "scholastic" works of Böhm-Bawerk. He

[1] See, George, Henry, *The Science of Political Economy*, New York, 1911, p. 103.

regrets that the science of Adam Smith, which was taught until 1880, has been abandoned. Severe as are his criticisms of the classical school, his own conception of political economy tends to be a continuation of the classical idea. He feels vaguely that only an inversion of end and means separates him from the "economists," whom he styles "scholastic." Making a detailed comparison between the social and the human body, George defines political economy as the science of the alimentation of the social body. Aside from Smith, it is especially to J. B. Say that he recurs to on this point. As a motto for book II of his *Science of Political Economy*, George cites Say's appreciation of Smith. Elsewhere he wrote, "Say's treatise on political economy, which being translated into English and widely circulated on both sides of the Atlantic, became for a long time, in the United States at least, perhaps the most popular of the expositions of the science that Adam Smith had founded."

Not only could George find valuable suggestions in Say, but, more than that, it is the French eighteenth century of which the American author foresees the perfection. This is shown even more by his method and his spirit than by his conception of political economy.[1] The plan of George's work shows his systematic tendencies. In general outline, his work recalls Carey; while in its wealth of detail, it reminds one of Daniel Raymond. Is not good terminology necessary? asks our ideologist. Words help us not only to express our thoughts, but help us to think. If political economy wishes to be a science, it must follow the deductive method. The facts which it comprises are too complex to lend themselves to an inductive method. As an example of lax method, George refers to Carey who, he alleged, made the mistake of joining deduction and

[1] Cf. George, *The Science of Political Economy*, pp. 35–6.

induction. Like J. B. Say, George believed it necessary to be able to distinguish what is essential from what is purely accidental. Moreover, although deduction follows the fundamental law of least effort, it may at the same time embody a great deal of historical color. Like Say, Carey, Bastiat, and Comte, George praises that type of reasoning which draws its illustrations from primitive and simple conditions and circumstances, because he believed that beneath the confusion of civilization, laws were operative which were fundamentally the same as those which governed simplified communities. The nineteenth century economists, said George, have by their analysis obscured phenomena which are clear at first view. He cites Turgot as an illustration of an economist who saw things clearly from the first and who did not confuse or bewilder his readers.[1]

Obscurity in political economy, according to George, is often willful and intentional. His experience with life had been too varied for him to believe that lack of clarity was always due to defects of the mind of the author. Under the pretext of profundity, said George, emerges obscurity in exposition which has its real origin in the defects of the heart of the author. Since the great struggle between men is for possession of wealth, would it not be irrational, George asks, to expect that the science which treats of the production and distribution of wealth should escape all the tarnishing influence of this struggle? The whole structure of political economy, said George, is admirably calculated to serve the powerful interests which dominate the universities. These interests, therefore, abhor a political economy which is simple and comprehensible. They wish to render the unfortunate students incapable of thinking

[1] George, *The Science of Political Economy,* pp. 72, 73, 98, 99; *Progress and Poverty,* p. 10.

upon economic subjects. George cites in this regard what Schopenhauer wrote of the works of Hegel. Whosoever accepts a chair in a university, George concluded, does it under the implied condition that he will never really find what it is his profession to seek. Unfortunately, the intellectual dishonesty which George denounced with such noble indignation, the perversion of mind which is the consummate perversion of the heart, still exists.[1]

In 1890, Henry George retraced his boyhood voyage to Australia. He died suddenly after his return to the United States, in 1897, at the age of fifty-eight years. Shortly before his death he had shown signs of considerable pessimism. "It seemed to him," wrote George's son, "that the century was closing in darkness; that the principle of democracy, which has triumphed in 1800 with the ascendancy of Jefferson, . . . might be conquered by the Hamiltonian principle of aristocracy and plutocracy in 1900." That intuition is the whole thesis of *Progress and Poverty*.

Section II

The Elements of the Problem of "Progress and Poverty"

It is neither standing armies nor customs duties, said Henry George; it is not deplorable political autocracy nor want of economic progress which breeds misery, because misery is to be found as wide-spread under a regime of democracy and free trade. Instead of decreasing with progress, misery is the very result of progress! The advance of invention has given men powers of which they dared not dream a century ago. But the machine mechanism, which economizes on labor, does not economize on the lives of children. Progress ceaselessly accentuates the

[1] George, *The Science of Political Economy*, pp. 33–4.

contrast between "the House of Have and the House of Want."[1] In old countries, in the midst of greatest abundance, exists the most severe want and penury, while in the transition of new countries into old is to be seen clearly how progress, instead of curing poverty tends to breed more poverty. Misery is in the process of migrating from Great Britain to the United States. Even now, people are beginning to recall the good old days of young America.

In brief, what dismayed George was not only the correlation between political progress and misery, but between misery and economic progress. Invoking, by way of Carey, the idea of Sismondi, he wrote: "to base on a state of most glaring social inequality, political institutions under which men are theoretically equal, is to stand a pyramid on its apex." But if the discord between political equality and social inequality is so striking, it is because of the interposition of an economic factor. If political progress is incapable of realizing social progress, it is because the economic progress which has taken place is not only unable to abolish poverty, but this economic progress itself incessantly breeds misery. This phenomenon, said George, is the great enigma of our time; "The promised land flies before us like a mirage."[2]

Section III

The Criticism of the Wages-Fund Doctrine

Why, asks George, despite the increase of production, is there a tendency of wages toward a minimum? The reply of classical political economy is the famous "wages-fund" theory. Wages are determined by the proportion between the number of laborers and the sum total of capital set aside for the employment of labor. If wages tend con-

[1] George, *Progress and Poverty,* p. 7.
[2] *Ibid.,* pp. 2–3.

stantly toward a minimum of subsistence, it is because laborers naturally multiply more rapidly than capital expands.

Both terms of this equation, which is presumed to determine wages, said George, are false. In the first place, there is no fund of capital especially set aside or destined for the payment of wages. In the second place, an unlimited increase of population, instead of reducing wages, can only increase wages.[1] In order to prove that there is no "wages-fund," George begins his exposition by defining precisely the fundamental concepts of labor, land, capital, value, and wealth.

Labor is defined as all human effort, manual or otherwise, exerted with a view to producing wealth. Wages, being that part of the product which goes to labor, includes all remuneration for such effort.[2] Land consists of matter and gratuitous natural forces.[3] Capital includes those things which are neither land nor labor but which result from the combined action of these two factors of production. Nothing can be capital which is not itself wealth. Therefore, in order to precisely define capital, it is necessary to define wealth, and in order to define wealth, it is first necessary to define value.[4]

George's theory of value is an amalgamation of most diverse ideas. Not only does he retain Adam Smith's distinction between "value in use" and "value in exchange" (confining "economic value" to exchange value), but besides that he attempts, as Smith did, to discover a fixed standard of value. This opposes him for the moment to J. B. Say. Value is not a relation, said George, of everything to every other thing, but of everything to one given

[1] George, *Progress and Poverty*, p. 9.
[2] *Ibid.*, p. 14.
[3] *Ibid.*, p. 15.
[4] *Ibid.*, p. 16.

thing which is the very source and measure of value. This measure of value is human labor. The successors of Smith have been mislead by the belief that it would be dangerous for social institutions to push inquiry too far on the subject of the fundamental principle of value. Value does not arise from exchangeability, but exchangeability arises from value. Value, in the final analysis, is the amount of labor which the possession of a thing permits one to save, or, according to Smith's phrase, to impose on someone else by means of exchange.

By virtue of the fundamental law of least effort, value, which is equal to the smallest quantity of labor possible, would appear to be essentially subjective. The point of equivalence, that one assumes when speaking of the value of a thing, is the point where the desire of acquisition on the part of the recipient is in equilibrium with the desire of the provider of the commodity for keeping it. Yet this necessary equilibrium, according to George, was the source of the "grotesque errors" of the Austrian school. In reality, George's conception of value is completely confused. Beginning with a rejection of "value in use," George ends with a recognition of the subjective character of value. In spite of himself, George was probably influenced by the neo-classical triumph. But the essential point of George's value theory is that value is the amount of labor which the possession of a thing permits one either to avoid or to make someone else perform.

This distinction allows one naturally to pass from value to wealth. Of the two elements which give value to a commodity, the first is a relation between man and things. This concept involves a technical point of view as well as a social point of view: value derived from a process of production which increases the common fund of wealth. The second element of value is quite different. This concept involves a relation between men, and views value from a legal point of view as well as an individual point of view, value being derived from the power which certain men have of substituting the labor of other men for their own labor. This power does not increase the common fund of wealth. The increase in the value of real estate is an excellent example of this latter process. The foregoing concepts of value and wealth can be traced not only to Carey and Raymond, but also to Say. The return to Say's theory, however, is only a return in a general sense, because Say repudiated the conclusions to which George's theory points. Although all wealth has exchange value, everything which has exchange value is not wealth, but only to the extent that it is derived from production; that is, to the extent that it is crystallized labor. There should be excluded, on the one hand, all non-material labor and all "immaterial products"; on the other hand, all matter available without labor, all free goods.

Although all wealth has exchange value, everything with exchange value is not wealth. Likewise, although capital is wealth, all wealth is not capital. Only that part of wealth is capital which is devoted to production and is not yet in the hands of the consumer. In short, capital is "wealth in the course of exchange," interpreting exchange not in the narrow sense, but expanding it to what Say called "the great exchange of production." In Henry George's theory, production, the relation of men to things, is what distinguishes value from wealth and wealth from capital. Value which proceeds from production is wealth; wealth which returns to production is capital.[1]

By aid of these definitions of his concepts, George undertakes to demonstrate that there is no such thing as a wages-fund of capital especially set aside for the payment

[1] George, *Progress and Poverty,* pp. 17, 18, 19, 20.

of laborers. He alleges that the classical theory rests upon a double optical error. It allows itself to be mislead, on the one hand, by the fact that wages are paid in money; on the other hand, by the fact that they are paid before the completion of the product upon which the labor is expended.

The fundamental truth to which one should adhere in all economic reasoning (as Carey, Bastiat, Raymond, and Say had done) is that a principle which applies to a primitive society applies with equal or greater truth to the most complex society.[1] A laborer who works for himself receives his pay from his own product. He pays his own wages. So does a laborer who is employed by someone else. If one looks at the problem from the social point of view, said George, the monetary veil which conceals the economic mechanism disappears, and one should recognize that wages no more come out of the capital of the employer than a check drawn by a depositor draws out a bank's capital. It may be objected that wages cannot be paid out of an unfinished product and that monetary wages, therefore, conceal an advance of capital. An objection without weight, said George. If any advance has been made, it is the other way around; a greater advance has been made by the laborer to the employer than from employer to laborer. Long as the complete process of production may be, the creation of value does not depend upon the completion of the product; the process is continuous (which J. B. Say had pointed out) in such a way that it is not necessary to put aside capital for the payment of wages, because the partly finished goods are exchanged as quickly and as readily as a finished product. If the finished goods are withheld from exchange, it is not as an employer of labor that the business man has need

[1] George, *Progress and Poverty,* pp. 10–11.

of capital, but for purposes of commercial speculation.[1]

Neither is capital, in George's opinion, a subsistence fund. A subsistence fund does not aid production. It is not "wealth in the course of exchange." Therefore, it is not capital. Men do not eat in order to produce; they eat because they are hungry! George subordinates production to consumption, but this subordination is qualified by the fact that consumption depends upon simultaneous production. George illustrates this by a now celebrated passage: "Here is a luxurious idler who does no productive work either with his head or hand, but lives, we say, upon wealth which his father left him securely invested in government bonds. Does his subsistence, as a matter of fact, come from wealth accumulated in the past or from the productive labor that is going on around him? On his table are new-laid eggs. . . . What this man inherited from his father and on which we say he lives, is not actually wealth at all, but only the power of commanding wealth as others produce it; and it is from this contemporaneous production that his subsistence is drawn." This passage illustrates George's separation of the legal aspect of wealth from its technical aspect, of strict exchange from productive exchange, of value from wealth. The consumption of the idler is no more drawn from capital than is that of a laborer; the idler's consumption is still drawn from labor, except that it is not *his* labor, but the labor of another. If a laborer's consumption is dependent upon his production, then, said George, it is only fair that an idler's consumption should be limited to his production! Everything comes back, or should come back, to an exchange of labor. The thousands of intermediaries who separate a mechanical laborer from an agriculturalist must be kept in the background. The labor actually ex-

[1] George, *Progress and Poverty*, p. 12.

pended in the production of a machine virtually produces the agricultural commodities upon which the machinist spends his wages.[1]

If capital neither provides a wages-fund nor a fund of subsistence, what function does capital perform? Capital assists labor in the production of wealth in two ways: it permits labor to increase its efficiency by a subdivision of tasks, and secondly, it helps labor to utilize the productive forces of nature. The first of these uses recalls Smith; the second Say. Raw materials are furnished by nature. Capital therefore provides neither wages, nor subsistence, nor raw materials, and cannot limit industry. The only limit to industry is access to natural resources. Capital can limit the *utilization* of raw materials and resources that is to say the productivity of industry. It only affects maximum wages, not minimum. George replaces a relation between capital and labor with a relation between land on the one hand and capital plus labor on the other. If we suppose for the moment unlimited natural resources, labor does not encounter an external limit in capital nor an internal limit within itself. The classical equation for the determination of wages is wrong in both terms. Since labor is its own "fund," the multiplication of labor does not diminish the fund, but rather increases it. The fund is least wanting.[2]

George resumes the refutation of the Malthusian theory which Carey had begun. Like his predecessor, George pointed out that multiplication bears a direct ratio to the inferiority or superiority of species. The subsistence of man comes from vegetables and animals whose rate of reproduction is high. Subsistence therefore increases more rapidly than population. An abundance of subsistence

[1] George, *Progress and Poverty,* pp. 26, 30, 31, 32, 33, 34.
[2] *Ibid.,* pp. 34, 35, 38, 39.

does not induce mankind to multiply more rapidly, but to develop (an argument found today in the writings of Hobson). For at the same time that man is a superior animal, he is also a transitional form of matter. We bring nothing into this world, and we carry nothing away when we leave. In the second place, human multiplication does not reduce subsistence, but increases it. Although the increase of population does compel recourse to poorer soils, it also increases productive power to such an extent that there is more than equal compensation.[1]

Here is the essential difference between Malthus and George. Malthus was basically in agreement with Say. Malthus stated that misery resulted from an insufficiency of production. Say logically insisted that misery could be overcome by increasing production. George reverses the reasoning and closes the circle. The increase of production, said he, is realized by an increase of population. In other words, Malthus held that misery resulted from an insufficiency of production in relation to population. Say believed that misery could be cured by an increase of production in relation to population. George insisted that misery could be overcome automatically by an increase of population in relation to production. But whereas George could explain misery in new countries by a theory of under-population (a scattered population being insufficient in that new country) does not this reasoning preclude him from solving the problem of poverty in old countries where even more abject misery co-incides with an abundant population and intensely developed production? George replied that it was not the retardation or absence of progress which breeds poverty, but the very advance of progress. Here he seems to return to a naturalism similar to that of Malthus. George admits that

[1] George, *Progress and Poverty,* pp. 40 ff.

Malthus was right in regarding human multiplication as the first cause of misery, but he alleged that Malthus fell into error by failing to perceive the intermediate cause. What makes the problem paradoxical is that it is not in weakening production, but by increasing production, that human multiplication augments misery. This is a proof that a new cause is interposed between the increase of production and the increase of misery, a new cause which is to be found in the distribution of the increased wealth which is produced.[1] In the unequal distribution of wealth is to be found the explanation of the correlation between minimum wages and maximum production, between progress and poverty! Wages do not come out of capital, this has been shown. We shall next see that interest is derived from labor. There is a connection between capital and labor, said George, but the relation is just the reverse of the classical belief.

Since there are three factors of production, land, labor, and capital, the product is partitioned into three corresponding shares. The laws of distribution are clearly laws of proportion, so connected with each other that if two parts are given, the third can be deduced. George's exclusion of profits as a distributive share is quite natural. Of the three divisions of profits: compensation for risk, wages of management, and the remuneration of capital, the last named is explained by interest, wages of management by wages, and, if one considers social relations in the aggregate, risk is eliminated.

Not content with confining the distributive shares to three, George by a strict gradation, presently reduces them to two. Labor is the initial active force. Land, however, is the condition, the matter, the very field of labor. The natural order of the factors of production is, therefore,

[1] George, *Progress and Poverty*, pp. 4, 5, 6.

land, labor, capital. Labor expended upon land can produce wealth without the aid of capital, and, in the inevitable progress of things, must indeed produce wealth before capital can come into existence. Capital must therefore consist of land and labor. Three types of production can, in reality, be distinguished: 1. adaptation or alteration of the form or the place of natural products; 2. cultivation or the utilization of vital forces of nature; 3. exchange, or the utilization of natural forces which vary according to time and place. Although civilization reveals a tendency of manufactures to increase in relation to agriculture, this less direct recourse to natural forces is more than compensated by a much larger indirect recourse resulting from the extension of exchange, both geographically and in time, by means of capital. It is precisely because the recourse to land is secondary and indirect, that capital partakes less of nature than of labor. If one remembers that it is not capital which employs labor, but labor which employs capital, it becomes clear that capital is not a fixed amount. Rather, it can always, by the play of value, be augmented or diminished, either by devoting more or less labor to the production of capital, or by the conversion of capital into wealth or wealth into capital. As a consequence, interest is tied to wages; it cannot follow its own bent, but is correlated with the movement of wages. In a society of Dick and Harry, the more Dick has, the less there is for Harry, and conversely. The relation between capital and labor, however, is quite different. Competition, said George, tends either to raise interest and wages together or to lower them together. Thus George goes beyond Carey and back to Raymond, confining distribution, in the final analysis, to wages and rent.[1]

[1] George, *Progress and Poverty,* pp. 55 ff.

Although capital, in George's theory, is bound up with labor rather than with land, is not labor, as a factor, subordinate to land? What is it that separates capital from land and connects it with labor? What causes interest to be based upon wages if wages, in turn, are based upon rent?

Since wealth is the result not only of labor, but of land, whatever be the product conjointly produced by labor and capital, these two factors together can receive as wages plus interest only as much of the product as these two factors could have produced upon an area of free land where there was no rent. Progress has led men to cultivate lands of different qualities. The same amount of labor applied to a superior quality of land yields a larger product than when applied to an inferior grade of land. Since the surplus resulting from the cultivation of a superior grade of land is rent, wages are equal to the product of labor on the margin of cultivation. This throws a flood of light on economic problems. In new countries where the value of land is least, the rates of wages and the rates of interest are high. In old countries, where the value of land is considerable, the rates of wages and of interest are low. If the value of land increases more than proportionally, all the gain of production is absorbed by rent, whereas wages and interest remain constant. If the value of land increases more than in proportion to the increased product of labor and capital, wages and interest fall. It is only when the value of land increases less than in proportion to the increase of productive power that wages and interest can rise. George's correlation of the laws of rent, wages, and interest is now evident. All three are deduced from the same fundamental principle: the satisfaction of wants at the price of least effort. In the last analysis, wages and interest are affected not by the increase of productive power, but by the increase of rent.[1]

Thus George replaces the classical relation between capital and labor by a relation between land on the one hand and capital plus labor on the other. In the solidarity which he establishes between labor and capital and in the connection between wages and interest, he approaches near to Say's doctrine and opposes that of Ricardo. This very point gives us a forewarning of the divergence between George and the Marxian socialists. The economic conditions of his country were such that the American revolutionary could not comprehend the already accentuated conflict between capital and labor in Europe, a conflict which was the very result of the classical relation expressed in the wages-fund which George sets about to destroy. For this reason, George's theory is very near to that of Say by virtue of the union which he establishes between capital and labor and by his recognition of a conflict between land, on the one hand, and capital plus labor on the other. This similarity is, however, only approximate. Whereas Say saw a conflict between the industrial class (entrepreneurs and their associated laborers) and the landed proprietors, this was because there lingered in the French economist's mind a memory of feudal rent, of legal rent, which led him, in combating landed property, to repudiate the interference of government in economic matters. George's attitude is quite different. To him, the land question resolved itself into the injustice of the private receipt of rent, and, although he repudiated the Ricardian relation between wages and interest, it is nevertheless the Ricardian idea of rent which he adopts.

Rejecting both the optimistic productivism of J. B. Say and the distributive harmony of Carey and Bastiat, George declares that it is not the increase of productive power

[1] George, *Progress and Poverty,* pp. 60 ff.

that affects wages and interest, but the increase of rent. It is not the size of the gross product that determines wages and interest, but the available net product. Here is the new cause which is interposed between the increase of production and the increase of misery. Basically, this idea is neither the "net product" of the Physiocrats nor rent in the Ricardian sense. There is a complete replacement of the classical relation (which was a relation between technical elements) by a new relation which is a relation between technical elements, on the one hand, and legal elements on the other. Wages and interest, said George, are not affected by the productivity of labor, but by rent, while rent, in turn, is affected less by the productivity of land than by the degree of its appropriation, by the existing degree of land monopoly. In short, George, who is differentiated from Say because his point of view is more economic than political, is differentiated from Ricardo because his point of view is more social than economic. Ricardo held that the landowners were guiltless, because it was not high rents which made prices high, but high prices which made rents high. George did not absolve the landowners of guilt. For while it was true that high prices led to high rents, it was the disharmony between private ownership of land and social integration which made prices high.

To say that wages and interest are low because rent increases is akin to saying that a boat moves because the paddle wheels turn. The real question is: what makes rents increase? George's answer was that the cause lies in the three aspects of material progress: the increase of population, technical organization, and social customs. When the increase of population augments the productivity of labor more than it compels recourse to inferior grades of land, wages fall relatively, but increase absolutely. This is a reversal of the distributive harmony of Carey and Bastiat. Contrariwise, when the increase of population does not increase productivity sufficiently to neutralize the fall of yields on the margin of cultivation, rents rise and wages fall not only relatively but absolutely. Nevertheless, even in this case, the gains made from the lands of superior grades largely compensate the losses on the inferior grades of land. The total production of wealth, in relation to the total expense of labor, is greater even though the distribution of this wealth is more unequal.

George always distinguishes between productive exchange and exchange in the narrow sense, between social conditions and individual, between technical and legal conditions. These distinctions save him from becoming involved in flagrant contradiction. We find him declaiming against Malthus that the increase of population always brings an increase in the productivity of human labor. Although, in certain cases, the increase of population does not permit the accrued productivity to neutralize the fall of yields on the margin of cultivation, this is a problem of distribution, not of production. Here is indeed a complex notion of productivity. The labor of a hundred men, other things being equal, produces much more than a hundred times what the labor of one man would produce, but the labor becomes not only more productive but more "effective." George, resurrecting Raymond's term by a complete reversal of meaning, implies that the increase of population augments not only quantitative productivity, but qualitative productivity; increases not only supply, but demand. George describes, at length, the arrival of the first settler in a new region, the evolution of a village into a town, of a town into a great city, such as San Francisco. Like another Rip Van Winkle, this first settler falls asleep. Meantime, he becomes a millionaire! The most expensive land in the world is not land of extraordinary natural fertility, but land whose value proceeds directly from the increase of population. Rent is less the effect of population upon the supply of land by the direct quantitative intervention of natural resources, than the effect of population upon supply by the indirect and qualitative intervention of demand. This represents the "commercial productivity" of land; a theoretical extension of rent thereafter subject to the law of supply and demand. By these various ways, the increase of population increases rent.

This first factor of material progress, increase of population, gives significance to the other two: technical organization and social customs. While the first effect of technical improvements, which economize on labor, is to increase the productive power of labor, the second effect is to increase rent by extending the margin of cultivation. For every increase in the productive power of labor widens the demand for land. When land is completely appropriated, as in England, or rapidly susceptible of appropriation, as in the United States, the final effect of machinery, which economizes on labor, is to increase rent without increasing wages and interest. This reasoning is exactly the reverse of the optimistic industrial philosophy of Say, Carey, and Bastiat. As to the third factor of progress, social customs; this also serves to increase rent. For the happy effects of political and intellectual improvements are always monopolized by the landed proprietors.[1]

Rent is more influenced, therefore, by the demand for land than by the supply. Yet it is not legitimate demand which chiefly influences rent, but a monstrous form of demand, land speculation. In stationary societies, cultivation is not extended to lower degrees of productivity until

[1] George, *Progress and Poverty,* pp. 80 ff.

it has exhausted the superior degree. In progressive societies, combinations of land-owners, speculating upon future increases in value, engross land and keep it unproductive. Hence in the United States, the settler must push farther and farther west. Speculation increases rent faster than the advance of progress. In consequence, wages decline both absolutely and relatively. The mechanism which automatically checks and limits speculation in commodities, namely, the increase of supply as a result of the rise of prices, cannot limit the speculative advance of land values, because land is a fixed quantity which no human power can increase or diminish. There is only one limit to the speculative rise of rent: the minimum required by capital and labor for engaging in production.

The speculative increase of land values, said George, is the very cause of economic crises. The monopolization of land, the rise of rent on land made infra-marginal by speculative monopoly of better grades diminishes the return to capital and labor, and slackens production. This stoppage of production at certain points is transmitted to other points in the form of a diminution of demand until the entire network of commerce and industry is paralyzed. A crisis of overproduction or underconsumption results, the definition depending on the point of view. The period of depression continues until either the speculative rise of rent is arrested or until greater production, due to an increase of population and machine methods, permits normal rent to reach the level of speculative rent, or lastly, until capital and labor will consent to produce goods for a more meagre return. Very probably all three causes contribute to producing a new equilibrium. But every new speculative advance of rent involves a new stoppage of production and the usual consequences.[1]

[1] George, *Progress and Poverty,* pp. 104–14.

Yet when the desire to consume more co-exists with the capacity to produce more, the industrial and commercial paralysis can be attributed neither to underconsumption nor overproduction. George adheres to Say's theory of markets. Money is an intermediary which must be kept in the background. The cessation of demand for certain commodities is, in reality, the curtailment of the supply of other commodities. The slackening is thereby spread through the whole network of production and exchange. "But," said George, "the industrial pyramid manifestly rests on the land."—a sentence which Carey might have written.[1] The fundamental occupations which create the demand for all others are evidently those which extract wealth from nature. If, therefore, we retrace the process from one point of exchange to another, the cause of diminished purchasing power rests ultimately in some obstacle which hinders labor from applying itself to land. This obstacle is none other than the speculative rise of rent, a veritable lock-out of labor and capital by the landowners.

Such is the economic theory of Henry George. After having criticized the problem presented by the classical writers and repudiated their solution of it, he seeks out new elements from which he derives two solutions to the problem of progress and poverty. The classical equation for the determination of wages (the wages-fund theory) he brands as false in both terms. Labor does not encounter an external limit in capital. Neither does labor find an internal limit within itself, because labor is its own fund, a fund which, instead of diminishing with the increase of population, tends to increase. As distinguished from Malthus and Say, George proclaims that misery can

[1] George, *Progress and Poverty,* p. 110.

only be overcome by an increase of population in relation to production.

Still this explanation which is adequate for a new country where population is insufficient, leaves unsolved the enigma of old countries where an abundant population and intense production brings about a misery more and more harrowing. The problem of *Progress and Poverty* is then presented. It is not the retardation of progress which breeds misery, but its very advance. This, in turn, indicates the solution of the problem. A new cause must be found between the increase of population and production and the increase of misery, between overproduction and underconsumption; a new cause which is to be found in the distribution of wealth. Because wages do not come out of capital, it does not follow that there is no connection between the two distributive shares of wages and interest. Only, the relation between them is just the reverse of the classical hypothesis; it is interest which is derived from labor. But if interest depends less upon nature than on labor, in the final analysis, labor is dependent upon land; interest is based upon wages, but wages are strictly dependent upon rent.

From this reasoning, we can understand how George replaces the classical relation between capital and labor with a new relation between land, on the one hand, and capital plus labor on the other. By the intimate solidarity which he establishes between capital and labor (in which idea he approaches Say's doctrine), he opposes himself at the same time to both Ricardian economics and Marxian socialism. Although he repudiates the Ricardian relation between wages and interest, he nevertheless adopts the Ricardian theory of rent. The new cause which is interposed between the increase of population and production and the increase of misery is that wages and interest are affected not by the increase of productive power, but by rent, not by a gross product but by the available net product.

Does that mean that we find in George either the "net product" of the Physiocrats or the Ricardian doctrine of rent? No indeed. For the classical relation between technical elements is replaced by a relation between technical elements, on the one hand, and legal elements on the other. Here we find George's fundamental idea which we have already seen shining through his criticism of the wages-fund. Whereas wages and interest are not determined by the productivity of labor, but by rent, rent itself is not determined by the productivity of land, but by the degree of its appropriation. Rent is, therefore, determined less by the supply of land than by the demand for land, and is less determined by legitimate demand than by the monstrous form which demand assumes, namely, speculation in land, the very cause of economic crises.

Thus while George shows, almost as Malthus did, that social evil is only the consequence of economic progress, contrary to Ricardo, he demonstrates that it is, nevertheless, only the artificial consequence of a natural law. George therefore diverges from the classical French view in holding that social evils cannot be corrected automatically by the play of economic laws. He diverges from the classical English view in holding that social evils are not at all the necessary consequence of natural laws. In other words, George tends to sanction social action, which was unnecessary in the minds of the French optimists, impossible in the minds of the English pessimists. George, however, retained the naturalism of both groups of writers, except that he reduced both the force and the domain of this naturalism by the annexation of a certain social rationalism.[1]

[1] George, *Progress and Poverty,* pp. 116, 117, 119, 120.

SECTION IV

The Socialization of Rent by a Single Tax on Land

In seeking the appropriate remedy for the evil which he had isolated, George begins by rejecting inadequate measures, such as, public action, co-operative action, or collective action. All these remedies would be erroneous because they presume that the conflict is one between capital and labor, whereas the real conflict is between land, on the one hand, and capital plus labor on the other.

Reduction of governmental expense is certainly desirable, but this cannot have any effect in eliminating dis-harmony while land monopoly exists. Contrariwise, all positive government action is not only inefficacious, but is also thoroughly dangerous, since it is prejudicial to private initiative. The spirit of socialism, which can only be an ardent religious faith, is absent and therefore any attempted public action would be a step backward, a return to tribal collectivism. The socialist ideal is a noble one and no doubt capable of realization; but one cannot create socialism over night. It must grow naturally. Society is not a machine, but an organism. The life of the whole is regulated by the life of its parts. From these reflections, we can understand how deep-rooted George's individualism really was, an individualism which makes the individual not only the end of society but the means.[1]

Will individuals then, in the absence of government action, voluntarily and naturally provide each other with mutual aid? Consumers' co-operation, said George, by eliminating intermediaries, can only reduce the cost of exchanging goods. Its effect upon distribution can be no other than that of technical improvements which ulti-mately end by increasing rent. Producers' co-operation

[1] George, *Progress and Poverty,* pp. 122, 123, 130, 131.

merely substitutes proportional wages for fixed wages. Its only advantage is that it renders the laborer more active and industrious. In other words, it increases the productivity of labor, operating in the same fashion as machinery and always contributing to the same result: the increase of rent.[1]

What about class struggle? Would not this method be preferable to mutual aid? Surely associations of workmen can raise wages, and do this neither at the expense of other workmen nor at the expense of capital but at the expense of rent. The strike does not really pit labor against capital, but laborers against landed proprietors. If the contest were between labor and capital, it would be more equal, because the power of resistance of capital is scarcely greater than that of labor. In the case of a strike, not only does the income from capital end, but the capital deteriorates. Thus a strike is disadvantageous both to capital and labor. It is a struggle which can only properly be compared with war.[2] Moreover, landowners would win!

Of all the proposed measures for combatting the rise of rent, the only one which has the merit of touching the source of the evil is a more general distribution of land, the development of small landholdings. Nevertheless, this remedy is scarcely more efficacious. Not only are large landholdings more productive than small, but wages are lower in France and Belgium (countries with small holdings) than they are in England. (This does not contradict George's thesis: that greatest productivity involves lowest wages, because we must not forget that this diminution of wages cannot be absolute, but merely relative.) [3]

[1] George, *Progress and Poverty,* p. 128.
[2] *Ibid.,* pp. 125 ff.
[3] *Ibid.,* p. 131.

By repudiating public action, George differs from Raymond; by repudiating co-operative action, he differs from Carey. By his rejection of collective action which dissociates capital and labor, he tends to be similar to his two American predecessors; but he diverges from both Raymond and Carey by his criticism of small landholdings. Still the remedy which George proposes is, in the final analysis, only the adoption of a particular form of public action which attempts to realize a certain degree of social co-operation by reducing landholdings in significance, if not in area. The appropriation of rent by society, said George, is the only remedy which is possible and just; possible as a means, just as an end.[1]

The means whereby rent can be appropriated by society would be a single tax on land. A fixed assessment, not capable of being shifted, this tax would be easy to collect and would provide the government with the largest net revenue. At first sight, this solution seems to be physiocratic. But does it countenance the same end? "As I am acquainted with the doctrine of Quesnay and his disciples only at second hand," wrote George, "I am unable to say how far his peculiar ideas as to agriculture being the only productive avocation, etc., are erroneous. . . . But of this I am certain . . . that he saw the fundamental relation between land and labor . . . and that he arrived at practical truth, though it may be through a course of defectively expressed reasoning." George said that he did not know any English writer who had understood the Physiocrats or had taken account of the truth which lay at the heart of their theory of the sole productivity of agriculture. It was, said George, a vision of the Ricardian doctrine of rent carried farther than it had been carried by Ricardo, indeed to its logical consequences. George

[1] George, *Progress and Poverty*, pp. 132–3.

proclaims that land is the foundation of the industrial structure of society. It is not the growth of towns which causes the rural districts to develop, but it is the development of the rural districts which stimulates the growth of towns. The essential cause of misery can reside in no other place than in the inequality of landed property, because land is man's habitation, the store-house from which his wants are satisfied, the very field of his labor! Whereas J. B. Say reacted, to a certain extent, against both the economic and legal aspects of agrarianism, George's position is quite different. Although he shows himself to be an enemy of landed property, it is to safeguard better an agrarian economy. In his enthusiasm for a national agrarian economy, he rises to poetical style. "On the land," said George, "we are born, from it we live, to it we return again, children of the soil as truly as is the blade of grass or the flower of the field. Take away from man all that belongs to land, and he is but a disembodied spirit."

Although George is now very near to the Physiocrats by reason of his *laissez-faire* policy, he reminds one of the Physiocrats even more (except for their theory of the sterile arts) by his fiscal policy. This fiscal policy is bound up with his preference for agriculture, an agragrianism based upon a profound naturalism which, in turn, is inseparable from extreme rationalism. In reality, George is a doctrinal descendant of the Physiocrats not only in his political theories, but also by his economic theories (adopted also under their positive and negative forms by Raymond and Carey) and, most of all, in his philosophy. We shall see that the end he hopes to reach, by means of the single tax, is the proof of his philosophical sympathy with the Physiocrats.[1]

[1] George, *Progress and Poverty*, pp. 160, 167.

Contrary to Raymond, George considers as inadmissible the legal distinction between real and personal property, between movable and immovable property. The only acceptable distinction is the one which Bastiat made (more or less following Say) between things which are the product of labor and things which are a free gift of nature. The legal mind sees the same real property in a house or in the land upon which it stands. Nevertheless, the former was produced by labor, and is wealth; the latter, which is a free gift of nature, is land. Human labor alone gives a title to individual property. Nature releases her gifts to man as a result of labor, and man by labor draws the substance of wealth from nature. From this necessary collaboration between land and labor, it follows that individual property in land denies to labor its own product. The landowner has a right neither to land itself, nor to the value which social integration adds to the land, nor to the improvements which are inseparable from land itself. In this last case, the individual right is fused with a community right: the smaller is melted down into the greater. Moreover, it is easy to determine the dividing line between individual rights and collective rights. The criterion is provided by value. The value of a piece of land measures the difference between that piece of land and every other which may be had for nothing; it measures the right of the community to a piece of land possessed by an individual. To recognize and permit the peaceful usage of land, according to priority of possession, in return for the payment of a rent in the form of a tax contribution to the public treasury, reconciles care of land improvement with a recognition of equal rights for all. Land, said George, has a social function. It is no more necessary to make a man the owner of land to induce him to improve it, than it is necessary to set fire to a house to roast pork.

It is only necessary to say to this man: "the whole product of your labor or of your capital expended upon this land will be yours." What is really necessary, wrote George (in the words of Say), is not property, but security. In short, the user of land should receive as a return only that amount which he would have received from the possession of land in the total absence of society.[1]

From a distinction similar to Bastiat's distinction: between nature, which creates gratuitous utility, and labor, which by creating onerous utility, alone creates value, George draws a different conclusion. To the extent that his conclusion leads him to condemn landed property, George tends to approach J. B. Say. We can now understand how the reduction of value to service, that is to labor (by which Bastiat thought he had controverted socialism better than Say did) becomes, at the hands of George, an argument for socialism in land. George represents the third step in the theory; the other two are found in the writings of Say and Bastiat. Value, in his opinion, is not a gift of nature nor the product of individual labor; it is the work of society. Yet in coming to this conclusion, George elucidates the theory of Say and Bastiat more than he makes an innovation. He terminates a spiral doctrinal evolution traced by the two French writers and by H. C. Carey. Say had demonstrated that, thanks to the collaboration of nature in the work of production, (the "grand échange" in which man tends to give less and less and receive more and more) social wealth is essentially natural wealth. This theory of an automatic shortening of progress Carey lays down as his fundamental thesis. Even Bastiat, after having distinguished "gratuitous utility" from "onerous utility" (the latter being the product of service, the substance of value and alone appropriable)

[1] George, *Progress and Poverty,* pp. 136 ff.

demonstrated that "gratuitous utility" tends to become more and more common. George's innovation is consequently more formal than real. He is in agreement with Bastiat in wishing to reduce private property to the product of individual labor. But whereas, for Bastiat, the appropriated product of individual labor was measured by value, for George, value, on the contrary, is the measure of what should be socially appropriable (since if this is not the gift of nature, it is at least the gift of society). This very difference between Bastiat and George tends to draw George's theory closer to that of J. B. Say.

Say's analysis of economic equilibrium, his fusion of utility and value, of value and wealth (by his simple distinction between the value of products and the value of services) really permits him to conceive of value not only as a gift of nature, but, exactly as George does, as a gift of society. Moreover, this amounts to the same thing, since the gift of society is the result of the more gratuitous collaboration of nature in the work of production. Social wealth is, therefore, largely a form of natural wealth. George, following back through the century to Carey and Bastiat, finally returns to Say himself, except that the part of the philosophy which was natural with Say becomes rational with George. The social gain, which Say believed would be spontaneously diffused in society, should, in George's opinion, be captured deliberately by society through the means of a tax which would condense the social gain in appropriable form. In reality, George's doctrine not only reaches back to J. B. Say, but to the Physiocrats (whom he surpasses in insight). One significant question now arises. Was George's rationalism a pure and simple revival of the natural law of the Physiocrats, or was it more akin to the obliteration of economic naturalism by the individual naturalism of

Rousseau? The Jeffersonian tendencies of Henry George and his inevitable lack of appreciation of enlightened despotism should give some intimation of the answer.

If social gain is shamefully engrossed by rent, the benefits of George's reform program should extend to the whole economic system. It should make for harmony within production, harmony between production and distribution, between distribution and consumption.[1] A land tax, instead of arresting production, would stimulate it by destroying speculative rent, which leads both to unused land and to economic crises. Production would be more active and would also be equilibrated with demand. Large landowners would suffer only a relative loss; they would receive an absolute gain. The principal burden of the single tax would fall upon urban land values rather than agricultural. Paradoxical as it may seem at first view, the effect of a tax upon land value would be to relieve the farmer of all tax burdens. He would only have to pay a tax when the concourse of people had given rise to a rent on his land. Besides, the disappearance of speculative land values would disperse the population from places where it was too dense and distribute it to places where it was insufficient. The people of the towns would partake of the pure air and the sunshine of the country. The people in the country would participate more in the social life of the city. With the extension of machine methods, population would tend to regain primitive village form.[2]

The socialization of rent, said George, would create harmony, not only between agriculture and industry, but also between production and distribution; not only between man and things, but between men themselves. Instead of competition between laborers, resulting in a

---

[1] George, *Progress and Poverty*, pp. 155–6.
[2] *Ibid.*, pp. 179 ff.

lowering of wages to a subsistence level, there would take place (similar to Carey's vision) an augmentation of wages due to competition between employers. Employers would have to contend not only with other employers, but also with the faculty which laborers would have of becoming their own employers. The natural relation of men to things would thereby be restored.[1]

Equilibrium within the domain of production, equilibrium between agriculture and industry, harmony between production and distribution; these were ideas cherished by Raymond and Carey. George's greatest innovation lies in the harmony which he hopes to establish between distribution and consumption; harmony in the relation between men. One part of produced wealth represents the effort of the individual; another part, gathered up in rent, in value, represents the assistance which the community lends to the individual. Of these two parts, the first would be distributed to individual producers in the form of wages and interest, in proportion to the rôle which each individual had played in the work of production. The second part would go to the community and would subsequently be distributed equally among its members, strong or weak, old or young. Whereas material progress tends to increase rent, the capture of this rent by the group would assure a more and more perfect equality. After having distinguished individual effort from social effort, George outlines a remarkable inversion. To individual effort there corresponds a social duty: each according to his capacity; to social effort corresponds an individual right: to each according to his need.[2]

What is the meaning of this double distinction? It is an adaptation of means to end. The only way to attain

---

[1] George, *Progress and Poverty*, p. 176.
[2] *Ibid.*, p. 177.

an individual right is first to raise one's self to the notion of a social duty. We have fallen into the bad habit, said George, of looking upon rapacity as the strongest of human motives. Whence comes this thirst for gain which leads one to disregard all that is pure and noble? Whence comes this avarice which destroys patriotism, which makes religion hypocrisy, and which transforms existence into a conflict whose weapons are violence and fraud? Does it not have its origin in want, in that physical misery which is also moral degradation? It is the spur of need which makes men admire fortune above all other things and leads man to adopt as his motto: make money, honestly if you can, but above all, make money! Man is a superior animal, an imperialistic animal. He seeks in wealth the power that it gives, the consciousness that it raises him not only above need, but above other men.[1]

It is precisely because man is not merely an animal that he will be able to raise himself above his selfish interest to his social duty, and from his social duty to his individual right. He will learn not to take advantage of another, nor of himself. The spectacle of men who have only a few years to live making slaves of themselves for the sole pleasure of dying rich is so absurd, so contrary to nature, that in a state of society where the abolition of poverty is the envious concern of the masses, whosoever tries to acquire more wealth than he can use would be regarded as much of a fool as a man who each day puts on a half-dozen hats. In contrasting Adam Smith with Mandeville, George concludes that it is a philosophy of narrow view which rests upon egotism. Personal interest is only a mechanical force. There is an organic force which is more powerful.[2]

[1] George, *Progress and Poverty,* p. 178.
[2] *Ibid.,* pp. 179, 186 ff.

Is it not, George asks, because the classical economists deny the moral qualities of man that they derive social evil from a natural law? Like Carey, George attacks the materialism of classical political economy; challenges that type of political economy called the "dismal science." This economic theory, said George, as it is taught, is certainly disheartening. But this is only because it has been degraded, because its truths have been corrupted, because its harmonies have been falsified. In reality, political economy radiates hope. It is impossible to conceive of a means without an end. The metaphysical necessity of perfectibility is so strong that those who accord only present life to the individual are constrained to transfer the idea of perfectibility to the race. Civilization is a progress not of man's nature, but of society. It has no fixed point, and can sometimes disappear. Had George's theory of evolution been on trial at Dayton, Tennessee, the case would have been promptly settled! If the classical writers derive social evil from natural law, said he, it is because they deny the moral qualities of man and because they misconstrue the true meaning of natural law and therefore base a false economic naturalism upon a false individual utilitarianism. As contrasted with the classical reasoning, George believed that once his ideas were put into practice the inequalities which would continue would be natural inequalities; not artificial inequalities which arise from a misunderstanding of natural law.[1]

Classical political economy appears to be economic naturalism based upon individual utilitarianism. From Rousseau to Say, the kindness of nature passes from the individual to society. Optimism goes from one extreme to another. The pessimism of the English classical school is a false return to the social pessimism of Rousseau. Al-

[1] George, *Progress and Poverty,* pp. 185, 189, 191, 207 ff.

though to a great extent defective, the economic organism remains, nevertheless, integrally natural. George has thus made a complete return to Rousseau: individual naturalism is the end of his social utilitarianism. We can now understand how what was purely natural with J. B. Say becomes rational with George. The social gain which Say believed would be spontaneously diffused in society, should according to George, be captured by means of a tax upon rent, which would condense the social gain for the benefit of the group. Individual utilitarianism is thus replaced by individual naturalism, while economic naturalism becomes social utilitarianism. Does George, by this philosophical metamorphosis, separate himself from the Physiocrats as well as from Say? Indeed not! Moreover, his ignorance of enlightened despotism is only a superficial difference, if one considers how near the concept of "droit naturel" is to Rousseau. This is indicated by the words of Bandeau, to which George enthusiastically subscribed: "We have a certain habit, we other economists, of beginning always by examining what is just, before seeking what is expedient."

Do we not find George regretting the disappearance of a state of nature? Do we not find him proclaiming that it is a strange thing that men who wish to labor in order to satisfy their wants, cannot do so? Anton Menger has therefore made a mistake in alleging that George did not derive the right to labor from the right to land. That is exactly what George did. Place man, he wrote, on a desert island and even though deprived of all the enormous advantages of co-operation and of the machinery of a civilized society, nevertheless, his two hands are sufficient to devise means whereby to cover himself and protect himself from cold. Is this not because man there has free access to the resources of nature which are afterwards closed to him? This naturalistic individualism which rises up against economic society recalls Rousseau's rebellion against political society.

George points out the analogy between the existing economic problem and the old political problem. If circumstances had focused the attention of the first English colonists upon landed property, it is very probable that they would have returned to first principles in this sphere as they did in the political. Private property would have been rejected along with monarchy and aristocracy. In their country of origin, however, the land system had not yet produced its full effect, and their new country was an immense continent with unlimited resources. Equality seemed sufficiently assured since the appropriation of land did not involve the exclusion of others. By this penetration of the economic sphere by the individual, by the application of social utilitarianism to individual naturalism, the socialism of George is similar to political revolutionary theory.[1]

What, in reality, is George's social utilitarianism? It is the penetration of politics by economics! George's return to the principles of Rousseau, instead of being simply circular, is rather the apex of a spiral evolution. If by the application of my ideas, said the American writer, the democratic ideal whereby government is abolished should be approached, it would only be the abolition of repressive political government. Under the socialist plan, the developing public powers would not fail to take public services in hand. Likewise, only by the trusteeship of the state could the increasing revenue drawn from the land tax be applied for common benefit: "Government would change its character and would become the administra-

[1] George, *Progress and Poverty*, p. 148.

tion of a great co-operative society." Whereas in classical economics, individual utilitarianism was the necessary means of economic naturalism, in George's socialism, social utilitarianism is the necessary means of attaining individual naturalism. The social ideal is the reinstatement of the individual in economic society by means of the preliminary penetration of politics by economics. Means must be provided for attaining this social goal, and these necessary economic means depend upon an enlightened political mechanism for their institution. When this is achieved, social equality and political equality will be co-existent. We now understand why George could glory in the famous text of the Declaration of Independence that "all men are created equal; that they are endowed by their Creator with certain inalienable rights; that among these are life, liberty and the pursuit of happiness."[1]

In short, having resolved the problem of progress and poverty, Henry George repudiated inadequate remedies and proposed as the sole valid remedy the "impôt fonciere unique" of the Physiocrats. George is the doctrinal descendant of the Physiocrats not so much in his political theory as in his economic theory, and even more in his philosophy than in his economics. In order to realize the social appropriation of rent by means of taxation, it is necessary to have recourse to value (which is the criterion which distinguishes the product of social integration from the product of individual labor). This notion of value brings George back to the doctrines of Carey and Raymond. Indeed it carries him back to Say, and from Say back to the Physiocrats. It goes even beyond the physiocratic doctrine of naturalism to a theory of rationalism. For George is not content to distinguish the product of

[1] George, *Progress and Poverty,* pp. 184 ff. and p. 198.

social effort from the product of individual effort. He sets up an ethical theory as well. With individual effort there corresponds a social duty: each according to his capacity; with social effort corresponds an individual right: to each according to his need. The only way whereby the individual right can be obtained is by first raising oneself to the notion of a social duty. Here is a severe criticism of classical political economy (which George alleged had fallen into the error of basing social evil upon individual fault). Only because classical political economy denies the moral qualities of man (by alleging that man is purely selfish) can it derive social evil from natural law. This is nothing less than basing a false economic naturalism upon a false individual utilitarianism. Without renouncing the physiocratic idea of natural law, George returns to Rousseau in making social utilitarianism take the place of individual utilitarianism.

To what extent is this idea of social rationalism a return to the political rationalism of Jefferson and Rousseau? Only to the extent that their end is the same, namely, individual naturalism. George, however, hoped to reach this end by different means: by social rationalism. The social goal is the reinstatement of the individual in economic society by means of a preliminary penetration of politics by economics. To accomplish this, economic means are necessary, but these very means are, in fact, a political end.

By this philosophical process, Henry George, after he has proved the discord between social progress and political progress, and after he has shown that this discord results from the interposition of economic progress, derives a social rationalism from his analysis of economic progress. This social rationalism indicates a return to political rationalism.

From Raymond and Carey to Henry George the American Reaction against Classical Political Economy Weakens in Form but Is Accentuated in Substance

The works of Henry George complete a remarkable evolution in the economic thought of the United States during the nineteenth century. Neither Raymond, Carey, nor George were professional economists. Raymond was a lawyer, Carey a business man, and George a "jack of all trades." All were self-taught. Yet in this succession may be traced the very evolution of America in the nineteenth century, from the *economic politics* of Raymond, to the *political economy* of Carey; from the political economy of Carey to the *social economics* of Henry George.

Raymond was primarily antagonistic to the doctrines of Smith and Say. Carey partially returned to the classical economics of Smith and Say in order to oppose the pessimism of Ricardo and Malthus. George tends to admit the classical pessimism, or at least the correctness of the Ricardian rent theory. Nevertheless, there were elements in the economic history of America which led George to refute the pessimism of Malthus' population theory. In spite of rapid immigration, labor was more and more necessary for America's growing industry; labor was still the short factor, although land was no longer the long factor. These economic conditions led George to resume the refutation of Malthusianism which Carey had begun. Under the sovereign influence of economic facts, George restricts the sphere of English economic theory by a rejection of the Malthusian theory of population, although he adopts the Ricardian theory of rent. By this qualified acceptance, George perverts Ricardian economics, regarded as a comprehensive system. The reaction against classical political economy therefore weakens in form, although it is accentuated in substance. All of which goes to show how economic facts influence economic theory.

Raymond's condemnation of "private monopolies" is the embryo of Carey's attack upon "trade" and finds complete development in George's criticism of the monopolistic tendencies of landowners. For all three authors, the economic structure of society should be agrarian. Carey looked forward to an harmonious combination of industry and agriculture; Raymond's interest in developing industry presumes agricultural predominance; George raised a cry of alarm lest industry should obliterate agriculture. Next to labor, land was the supreme factor of production and should share fiscal obligations with labor. The three writers are also in agreement in basing capital upon labor and restricting distribution to wages and rent. With disgust, George repudiates the pretended predominance of capital over labor. Many other elements are common to the theories of the three writers: the same opposition between legal and technical factors; between exchange in the narrow sense and the "exchange of production"; between the individual and the social point of view; between the relation of men to things and the relation of men to other men. There is also the same distinction between value and wealth, a distinction which for both George and Carey represents a more or less confused expression of J. B. Say's favorite idea of the automatic abbreviation of economic progress.

One would fall into grave error, however, if he should fail to perceive a significant evolution beneath this striking similarity between the economic theory of Raymond, Carey, and George. It is true that George, like Raymond, speaks of "effective labor"; but unlike Raymond and unlike Carey he means by this expression not quantitative productivity, but qualitative, not the creation of wealth, but value, not supply but demand. The whole idea is completely reversed. This illustrates the influence of facts upon the permanence of ideas. Although George has apparently rejected both the productive emphasis of Say and Raymond and the distributive harmony of Carey and Bastiat, he cannot separate himself from the persistence of the French ideas.

The upshot of George's rationalism (by which he attempted to repudiate the English naturalistic substance and the French naturalistic form of political economy) is that it infuses into the English form of economic theory the French substance. By admitting the predominance of demand (which seems to differentiate George from his Franco-American predecessors) George perverts the Ricardian theory of value and distribution. Although wages and interest are affected less by the productivity of labor than by rent; rent, in turn, is affected less by the productivity of land than by the degree of its appropriation; less by supply of land than by demand for land. This is neither more nor less than Say's conception! To George, however, it is social demand which was of importance. Value is not a gift of nature, as Say asserted; neither is it the product of individual labor, as Bastiat alleged; it is the work of society. On the spiral of doctrinal evolution, George's position corresponds to that of Say, except since the evolution has been in spiral form, it is above and beyond that of his French predecessor. In Say's theory, it will be remembered, the influence of supply is progressively superseded by the influence of demand, precisely because a social gain results from the increased collaboration of nature in the process of production. Man receives more gifts from nature, and social wealth tends more and more to be reduced to natural wealth. Carey made this theory of automatic progress his fundamental thesis. George, on the contrary, believed that progress would have to be directed and governed. The social gain which Say believed would be naturally diffused in society, George thought would have to be partitioned purposefully. It should first be gathered up by a tax upon rent which would condense the social gain in distributable form. Herein lies George's rationalism. It reaches back farther than to J. B. Say, in fact to the rationalism of the Physiocrats and of Jefferson and Rousseau. It has its roots in that optimism which is less a given fact than an ideal to be realized.[1]

Section VI

George Rejects the English Naturalistic Substance of Economic Theory

George's rationalism is a repudiation of both the English naturalistic substance of political economy and the French naturalistic form. The consequence of this rationalism is that it introduces into the English form of political economy the French substance. Still this was not exactly innovation, since it continues a tradition whose origin can be traced both in England and in France.

The first logical reaction against Ricardian economics in England was that of a group of economists who had come under the French influence of J. B. Say and Destutt de Tracy. Among these was Samuel Bailey who, against De Quincey, criticized the labor theory of value, widened the concept of rent, and emphasized the time factor. Another member of this group was Lloyd who, as early as 1834,

[1] Cf. Sherwood, Sidney, *Tendencies in American Economic Thought*, Johns Hopkins University Studies, 1897. Cf. also Chinard, G., *Jefferson et les Idéologues*, Paris, 1925.

presented a first sketch of marginal utility. There was also John Rooke who, after having repudiated both the labor theory of value and the Malthusian relation between subsistence and population, emphasized the benefits of machinery as providing the means of obtaining increased wealth and cheaper commodities. Mountifort Longfield and Isaac Butt were also critics of Ricardian economics. They admitted the Malthusian analysis but tempered it with thorough optimism. In this, they remind one of the fashion in which Say thought he followed Malthus. Wages and profits are derived from productivity, and the increase of capital tends to lower the rate of profits. Productivity is always enhanced by the division of labor and by the use of machinery; the benefits thereof extend to agriculture as well as industry.

George Ramsay also popularized French doctrines in England. In his writings, we find the distinction between changes of form and changes of place, drawn from Destutt de Tracy, which Carey was later to make famous. Ramsay adhered also to Say's conception of the entrepreneur and of profits; emphasized the time factor and showed that rent is not only the effect of price, but the cause. Ramsay's work is English in inspiration only by his rejection of immaterial products. He gave his country a pregnant admonition when he wrote, "Malthus has remarked, that it cannot be considered a natural, that is, a permanent state of things, for cotton to be grown in the Carolinas, shipped for Liverpool and again exported to America in its finished condition. The time must come when the United States will fabricate for themselves." [1] Finally, this group included Samuel Road who contrasted Smith (whom he admired) with Ricardo (whom he opposed).

[1] Ramsay, George, *An Essay on the Distribution of Wealth,* London, 1836, p. 496.

Road was an optimist who had faith in capital and in the entrepreneur. His essential critical contribution was that he recognized that the rising tide of socialism was connected with the Ricardian philosophy. This led him to make some notable social concessions, although he was a conservative. His chief proposal was a "land tax" representing twelve per cent of the rent. In spite of this crude formula, Road must be regarded as one English writer who wished to make of political economy not only a science of what is, but an art of what ought to be.

English socialism developed as a complex reaction against the optimism of those economists who wished to adhere to the doctrines of Adam Smith or of J. B. Say and to oppose the pessimism of Ricardo and Malthus. Yet a reaction against Smith and Say is to some extent a return to Ricardo and Malthus from whom the socialists adopted their pessimism. It was because the socialists considered this pessimism as a pure expression of facts that they were disgusted with the flagrant disagreement between Ricardian deductions (which they accepted) and their own notions of justice. In their quest for a theory of economic justice, however, the English socialists did not derive it from Smith or Say; rather they derived it, by way of Smith, from the Physiocrats. Here is just another example of the doctrinal entanglement of which Adam Smith is the center. If English socialism derived less direct influence from Robert Owen than indirect influence from Ricardo, perhaps it derived less from Ricardo than it did from Adam Smith and the Physiocrats. At least, it is important to understand how English socialism, whether it be optimistic or pessimistic, is as legitimate a descendant of Smith and the Physiocrats as classical political economy is. Under a more or less cut and dried Ricardian form, socialism has its roots in the doctrines of the fathers of political economy. In this Ricardian form and in this physiocratic-Smithian substance, it anticipates the theory of Henry George.

George's philosophy is strangely similar to that of Godwin, whose theories Raymond formally rejected. It is akin also to the ideas of Henry Hall who, more discerning than Godwin, had denounced the imposture of American liberty. To him, this so-called political liberty contained in itself the seeds of a future economic autocracy. Anticipating George, Thomas Paine demonstrated in a comprehensive fashion that progress breeds misery. Other English writers foreshadow George's social economics: Thomson and Gray, adhering to the distinction between productive and unproductive classes, helped turn the emphasis of English political economy from commerce to industry, from production to distribution; Patrick Colquhoun, by 1814, provided socialism with its statistical instrument; while John Bray had an influence on Marx which is particularly clear. Thomas Hodgskin developed the anarchistic vein of English socialism, which he derived from the Physiocrats through Adam Smith. He anticipated Carey's return to Smith and George's return to the Physiocrats. The part of Smith's theory which most impressed Hodgskin was the distinction in Book III of the *Wealth of Nations* between "human institutions" and the "natural order of things." In a cogent sentence, which either Raymond, Carey, or George might have written, Hodgskin said that Smith had carefully distinguished the natural distribution of wealth from distribution which proceeds from the artificial rights of property. Smith's successors, said Hodgskin, have not made this distinction, and in their writings, the effects of this right of property are considered as if they were the results of natural laws.

One other English writer who was similar to Henry

George, as well as to Villeneuve Bargemont, was Percy Ravenstone. Is not political economy questionable, he asked in 1821, when in the heart of the richest countries there reigns the most sordid misery? He anticipated Marx by proclaiming that rent and interest are predatory deductions from value which labor alone has created. Unlike Marx, however, Ravenstone made rent rather than interest the chief deduction. This attitude of Ravenstone symbolizes all the English economic thought in which the Ricardian theory of rent existed side by side with the Ricardian theory of value. J. S. Mill's work was a premature synthesis. While Marx openly opposed the rationalistic French tradition, Mill attempted to fuse the various currents into one large conciliation of individualism and socialism. Mill, as contrasted with George, did not believe that the whole potential social gain was to be found in the confiscation of rent; his scheme comprehended merely the socialization of future rent. Moreover, Mill did not conceive of a tax upon rent as the unique means of bringing about a reconciliation of individualism and socialism. As long as economic conditions in England placed emphasis upon a strict connotation of rent, little room was afforded for a theory of agrarian socialism; as soon, however, as these conditions were modified, it was a particularly favorable soil that the agrarian socialism of Henry George was to find in England. This does not mean that a most generous reception had not been prepared for George's doctrine elsewhere by such writers as Say, Saint-Simon, Proudhon, Colins, Huet, Renouvier, Fouillée, and Secrétan. Moreover, in 1851, Herbert Spencer had published his *Social Statics*, the only work whose influence George admitted. This book carries on a tradition which really goes back to the eighteenth century.

After 1880, English Social Christianity, which easily displaced Marxism, became the means of disseminating Henry George's ideas. Hyndman's book appeared, in 1881, and provided a literary means whereby George's ideas penetrated Social Christianity in England. Single tax leagues were formed in Great Britain, in Australia, as well as in the United States. Moreover, fiscal legislation in Germany, as well as in France, realized, more or less, the idea of a land tax, while in South America, George's socialism gave new life to the old emphyteutic system proposed for the Argentine by Rivadavia in 1826. Curiously, the modern Georgian liberalism of South America, quite contrary to George's theory, repudiates all socialism. It adheres strictly to orthodox economics. It confines its object to a single tax; landed property being for it the only evil which affects the economic organism.[1] Economic conditions of new countries always tend to make rent and the unearned income an extremely significant problem. All these details allow us to understand how essentially American is the work of Henry George, for it is, at the same time, retrograde and advanced; it is bound up with the past and with the future. The idea of a single tax expanded geographically rather than chronologically although the latter may follow. While the youthful Argentine Republic devised a single-tax policy before George's theory existed, old England had meantime conceived the theoretical necessity of the single tax by planting a seed which economic circumstances in America would indubitably nurture.

After 1884, the Fabian Society, although not yet willing to discard the theoretical imprint of Ricardo, at least, renounced the Marxian labor theory of value. Rent, in the Fabian theory, extended from land to capital and to human talents. By its rejection of Marxian theory, the

[1] Baudin, L., "Notes sur L'Amérique du Sud," *Revue D'économie politique,* (Jan.-Fev.) 1925.

Fabians also rejected Marx's social doctrine. They advocated no class struggle. For the time being, the existing bourgeois society should be continued. Meantime, policy should aim at general social interest; public, collective, and co-operative action should be combined. The result would be the slow but constant introduction of socialism. Wholesome optimism replaces Marx's pessimism, while the economic theory, the social doctrine, the very philosophy of Karl Marx is repudiated. Conversely, it is in close agreement with Henry George that Webb has written that the economic aspect of the democratic ideal is, in fact, socialism itself. This emphasis on the economic aspect is only a spiral-like return from social considerations to political. It is, of course, a political task on a higher level, since it comprehends the welfare of the group; passionate naturalism is replaced by social rationalism. For Karl Marx, the invasion of the political sphere by economic factors was an end in itself and his philosophy therefore concludes with the fatal economic naturalism of Ricardo. It fails to conceive of the re-instatement of individualism within the economic structure of the state. It fails to recognize that social utilitarianism should have individual naturalism as its goal.

In George's theory of socialism, the Ricardian theory of value disappears before the Ricardian theory of rent. This separates Anglo-Saxon from German socialism. The pessimistic Ricardian theory of rent, however, is in turn replaced by optimistic rationalism. Individual utilitarianism gives way to social utilitarianism and social naturalism to individual naturalism. By this new emphasis and by this new goal of socialism, Anglo-Saxon socialism is drawn nearer to the French tradition. Henry George, by way of his influence upon the Fabian Society completed the synthesis which J. S. Mill had been able merely to outline.

In Henry George's theory the divergent roots of the physiocratic-Smithian doctrines; optimistic, pessimistic, and socialistic are united in a theory of social economics.

In consequence of this doctrinal metamorphosis, the fundamental physiocratic tradition has assumed a Ricardian form. The formal English notion of rent has been expanded to include the French idea of social gain. This historical confluence of the English doctrinal tradition and the French doctrinal tradition represents also a perfect theoretical reconciliation of individualism and socialism. By developing the social aspects of rent, it has become possible to extend the English doctrine of rent in a theoretical sense. Conversely, this theoretical extension of rent has brought the French rent concept to its social extension. The significance of this complex movement is great. It holds forth hope for a rebirth of political economy. While the socialists see in both interest and rent incomes derived without labor, the economists who follow George see in rent a device which will bring to the members of society an income without labor. For rent in this larger sense is caused by demand. Since social demand is the cause of this income, rent will emerge, but this social product will be partitioned by the state: to each according to his need.[1] The socialist ideal will then have been reached.

SECTION VII

George Rejects the French Naturalistic Form of Economic Theory

As compared with the English doctrine, George's rent theory extends the meaning of rent from the social to the

[1] Cf. Menger, A., *The Right to the Whole Product of Labor,* London, 1899. See also Seligman, E. R. A., "On Some Neglected British Economists," *Economic Journal,* Sept., 1903.

theoretical sphere; as compared with the French doctrine of rent, George's doctrine of rent is extended from the theoretical sphere into the social. Through J. B. Say, he recurs to the eighteenth century Physiocrats.

George reminds one of the extreme individualism of his French contemporary, De Molinari. Both George and De Molinari felt that man's power over himself had not increased in proportion to the increase of man's powers over things. There are differences, however, as well as similarities. George's theory was based upon democratic political theory; in this, he differs from De Molinari. George believed that democracy and socialism were inseparable; here he differs from Guyot, from Sismondi, and from Villeneuve-Bargemont. Guyot, for example, believed that democracy would exclude socialism. Sismondi and Bargemont accepted socialism, but like De Molinari rejected democratic political theory. It is rather curious to find the advocates of budding socialism and declining individualism both reproving democratic political theory. The advocates of socialism believe that democratic government is inseparable from economic individualism. Conversely, the advocates of economic individualism regard democratic government as bound up with socialism. What Henry George did was to fuse together the economic individualism of De Molinari, the democratic political theory of Guyot, and the socialism of Sismondi and Bargemont. This means that George is related to that branch of French economics which goes back through Christian socialism to Saint-Simon and Proudhon. George's socialism is pre-Marxian: rationalistic, humanistic, and universalistic. We find in George some evidence of what we find in Proudhon: a criticism of both liberalism and socialism, an attempt to reconcile liberty and justice. Marx put George and Proudhon in the same category. Coming down to the present, George's work finds an echo in Landry, whose socialism is characterized by the predominance of demand; in the idealism of Malon, Berth, and Andler; in the rationalism of Renard, in the synthesis of Jaurés.

The synthetic method of George (which is characteristically French) is the method of Leon Walras. The latter conceives, as Gossen did, of an alliance between individualism and socialism which is strangely similar to that of George. In Walras' opinion, the state and the individual are only two abstract terms by which we designate the social man, depending on whether we consider him in the pursuit of his collective interests or in pursuit of his personal interests. The state is responsible for the common conditions of well-being; the individual is responsible for personal well-being. The consequence must be equality of conditions coupled with inequalities between persons due to personal differences. All revenue from social progress should accrue to the state, rent, for example. To the individual should be guaranteed the income from his labor and from his saving.

With Walras, as with George, the means whereby the reconciliation between individualism and socialism should be effected is the social appropriation of rent which is presumed to crystallize the social gain in appropriable form. But whereas with George the mechanism was to be fiscal (a single tax), with Walras the method should be land nationalization; pure and simple expropriation. The Lausanne economist did not distinguish between earned and unearned income from land. All income from land is legitimate, except that it is only socially legitimate. Here we find the contrast with the Anglo-Saxon economists. The latter carried the doctrine of rent from its social to its theoretical extension. Walras, on the contrary, carried the doctrine of rent from its theoretical to its social extension. His work recognizes implicitly the necessity of social equilibrium within economic equilibrium. In this idea Leon Walras goes back beyond his father, Auguste Walras, to J. B. Say, although whereas Say treated political and social problems as pure economics, Walras ends by treating pure economics as social economics. Here is the whole trend of French economic thought.

By these multiple bonds, Henry George's economics is connected with the French tradition. Embracing individualism and socialism, George's theory goes back beyond Walras, beyond Bastiat, beyond the Franco-American tradition, and finds its roots in the classical doctrine of J. B. Say. We need only recall Say's criticism of the Ricardian theory of rent: if the Ricardian idea of differential rent rests upon a misunderstanding of the essential distinction between rent and the profits of agriculture, in short, upon a misunderstanding of the functions of the entrepreneur, the Ricardian theory of monopoly rent rests upon a misunderstanding of the essence of value; namely, demand. George substitutes society for the entrepreneur (whom Say considered as the representative of society), and, like Say, emphasizes the predominance of demand. According to Say, it is by a slow transition that the net product of the landed proprietor passes to the entrepreneur and from the entrepreneur to society. George, who was influenced by the precipitous evolution of American economic life, would abruptly capture the net product of the landed proprietors for the benefit of society. Thus although the method differs, the philosophy is the same and this sentence from Say is the proof: "The landed proprietors are easily persuaded that the advantages which they draw from local circumstances are natural advantages which one has no more right to remove than one has a right to remove the fertility of their soil; but the right which other proprietors have of profiting from all the advantages which result from the progress of society, the right which consumers have of enjoying all the perfections of the art of production are rights no less sacred."[1]

George agrees with Say in recognizing both the static predominance of demand and also its dynamic predominance. Say rejects not only differential rent and monopoly rent, but their very foundation, the law of diminishing returns. For George, although there is "poverty," there is "progress" none the less. George completes a turn in the spiral of doctrinal evolution. He returns to Say, but meantime the theory has advanced to a higher level. He is similar to Say, because he recognizes that demand progressively supersedes the influence of supply and because like Say, he believed that "progress" means a larger social gain resulting from the more generous collaboration of nature. The social gain, however, must not be engrossed by land-owners; it must be captured by the state for the group. In the spiral evolution of doctrine, he is therefore compelled to return to government action. Herein he differs from J. B. Say.

Carey accepted Say's theory of automatic abbreviation of progress (due to increased collaboration of nature) as his fundamental thesis. George admitted the theory, but believed that the benefits of progress would have to be assembled and partitioned by state action. He thereby denies Say's naturalism and returns to eighteenth century rationalism. And although George follows the English tradition of proceeding from the social extension of rent to its theoretical extension, he is connected even closer to the Franco-American tradition in proceeding from the theoretical extension of rent to its social extension. In doing this, he goes beyond the rent theory of J. B. Clark.

[1] Say, *Cours d'économie politique pratique,* Paris, 1840, vol. ii, p. 98.

Clark's writings mark the beginning of a new period in the history of American economic thought. Although Clark had studied in Germany, he has himself admitted that he was no less indebted to the Franco-American doctrinal tradition of Destutt de Tracy, Say, Bastiat, Raymond, Carey, and George. His organic conception of society recalls both Raymond and Say. The great fact that society is an organism, said Clark, has been forgotten, and one is only concerned with individuals and their acts of exchange. Indeed Clark placed himself squarely within the Franco-American tradition when he wrote, "Society, as an organic whole, is to be regarded as one great isolated being; and this being may and does measure utilities like a solitary tenant of an island."

By this type of simplified reasoning, whereby social matters are reduced to individual matters, George had concluded that wages equal the product of labor on no-rent land. Clark admitted that he was thereby led to separate the product of labor from the product of the other factors of production. Clark concedes to George's theory absolute historical truth and relative theoretical correctness. It expresses a reality while free land still exists; it illustrates a tendency after land has been taken up: that wages tend to equal the product of labor. Clark generalizes the analysis by passing from a "margin of cultivation" to a "margin of utilization"; from agriculture to industry; from no-rent land to a "zone of indifference" (where the laborer receives the whole product of his labor). In short, the law of wages is a tendency of wages to equal the marginal product of labor and that labor is marginal which is applied at the zone of indifference. The Clarkian theory postulates the following mechanism: given a certain quantity of capital, there is a diminishing return from the labor which is applied to it; because of competition, no laborer can receive more than the marginal laborer; the surplus productivity of infra-marginal laborers is a rent which is due to capital. Conversely, given a certain quantity of labor, there is a diminishing return from the capital which is applied to it; because of competition, no increment of capital can receive more than the productivity of the marginal increment; the surplus productivity of the infra-marginal increments is a rent which is due to labor.

The Clarkian analysis restores the relation of men to things, but it is the lowest point in the scale of diminishing returns which governs remuneration. Wages depend upon marginal productivity. As a result, rent is inevitable. This generalization of rent, however, implies a kind of social compensation; the pessimistic rationalism of Henry George gives way to Clark's optimistic naturalism. Whereas George would socialize rent, Clark merely generalizes rent. Clark would neither go as far nor as fast as Henry George. For this reason, his doctrine may be said to be a renascence of Ricardianism.[1]

This theory of marginal utility of the American Neo-Classical school has several interesting characteristics. In the first place, by discovering no-rent land within a most complex economic structure of society, it again places man face to face with nature. In the second place, it definitely limits the French tradition by its return to the Ricardian principle of marginal productivity. Its third characteristic is the fact that the French tradition finally separated itself from the Ricardian error by shifting the emphasis in the marginal idea from supply to demand, from productivity to utility.

[1] Clark, J. B., *The Philosophy of Wealth*, Boston, 1886, pp. 4, 6, 9, 13, 14, 19, 22, 23, 25, 26, 37, 39, 41, 48, 51, 56, 58, 59, 60, 61, 62, 64, 65, 74, 76, 81, 82, 85, 86, 87, 88, 90, 97, 102, 160; *The Distribution of Wealth*, New York, 1924, pp. 2, 3, 10, 12, 19, 20, 21, 23, 24, 25, 26, 27, 30, 32, 33, 37, 38, 47, 50, 52, 60, 78, 88, 90, 93, 100, 102, 104, 113, 123, 124, 125, 139, 160.

Consequently, it is not only the Neo-Classicism of Jevons, Walras or Menger which represents a renascence of Continental economics and more especially French thought. The intermediation of Raymond, Carey, and George had an effect upon J. B. Clark. If the similarity between Bastiat and Carey demands something more than plagiarism to explain it, the same thing is true of a later simultaneous theoretical movement which was common to several countries. It was more than a mere co-incidence. It is a matter of an old tradition flourishing anew under the nurturing pressure of facts and ideas. A co-incidental enunciation of similar ideas in different countries, once seemingly inexplicable, has thus become abundantly clear in time.

In an epoch of great economic transition, the vicissitudes of his life suggested to Henry George the elements and the solution of the problem of *Progress and Poverty*. There is a discord, said George, between political and social progress which is caused by economic progress. Harmony can only be restored by means of social rationalism and a certain return to political rationalism. The theoretical essence of this rationalism, by which George repudiates both the English naturalistic substance and the French naturalistic form of economic theory, is the introduction of the French substance of political economy into the English form. By this means, George prepares the way for two things: communism and socialism, and a reborn political economy.

CHAPTER IV

THE CYCLE OF AMERICAN ECONOMIC THOUGHT

Since every final point is only suspension, every conclusion is relative, implying retrospect and prospect. One cannot trace a past evolution without indicating the trend of present evolution.

In very briefest form the trend of American economic thought in the nineteenth century was an abandonment of the French form of economic theory for the English form and a relinquishment of the English substance in order to develop the French substance. In the process of this metamorphosis, American thought, rather than passively submitting to the action of facts, reacted against facts.

The present American trend is rather different. Whereas American economic policy has been comparable with that of Germany, American economic thought tends again to resemble the English. List's system emphasized the political retardation of Germany; Raymond's theory emphasized the economic retardation of the United States. Yet American protection has been justified less and less by economic conditions and more and more by political considerations. In these political considerations are to be found the explanation of the definite change in the trend of American economic thought since the days of Henry George.

The French tradition in economic thought has been superseded in America by the English tradition. Physiocracy has given way to mercantilism (against which the American colonies revolted). Individualism and imperialism have disintegrated the body of thought which runs from Raymond and Carey to Henry George. The twentieth century has ground to pieces this nineteenth-century body of thought under the harshness of facts. One must admit, wrote J. B. Clark, in 1904, if not the definitive failure of democracy, at least its momentary eclipse. The United States has lost the vision of the stationary state. It has been seized by the frenzy of action. Like a great spinning top, the stability of the United States depends upon its movement. Only average individualism is developed in this paradise of bourgeois Victorian political economy. Centralization has all but killed the individual states of the Union and a narrow nationalist soul animates a continent. Only a false democracy has been preserved from the days of the American Revolution, a narrow rationalism of equalitarianism and standardization. Thought has become servile to facts. In this, it differs from the intellectual boldness which was characteristic of Henry George.

Modern economic thought is permeated with English Neo-Classicism. Taussig is the Marshall of the United States. Ricardian economics is still vigorous, not so much because it is Anglo-Saxon as because the economic evolution of America has followed and overtaken that of England.[1]

Although Marshall is covered with honor, Menger is preferred to Jevons who unfortunately chose to follow the French tradition. Indeed this preference indicates a second trend in modern American thought: a preference for the Austrian psychological school rather than the French mathematical school. The former is individualistic as contrasted with the emphasis on the social significance of economic equilibrium of the mathematical school. American economic thought has not turned to psychology as a reaction against the materialism of practical life (as is commonly believed in France); it has instead turned to

[1] *The Trend of Economics,* New York, 1924.

psychology under the very action of this practical life to avoid condemning it. Indeed this trend is, to a great extent, a scientific subterfuge! By means of psychology is sought the exclusion of social considerations and the restriction of economic theory to the individual. Mathematics is restricted to a methodological device.

A third characteristic of modern American thought is the statistical emphasis, which is truly American. In the United States, statistics play a double rôle. As a plain expression of facts, they are an essential element in the capitalist technique, the means whereby big business utilizes a more and more social economic structure for private ends. Although a natural derivative from facts, statistics are applied as an artificial rule of mind, since they simultaneously comprehend the individualistic and quantitative point of view. Social considerations tend progressively to be excluded. American economists in the nineteenth century began to speak of "economics" instead of "political economy" and thereby raised the indignation of Henry George. Today "business" has taken the place of "economics," a change of nomenclature which has provoked the penetrating criticism of Thorstein Veblen.

A fourth element in modern American thought is the historical current, the German tradition manifesting itself in "institutional economics." The influence of the German Historical School, toward the close of the nineteenth century, was particularly strong, precisely because American economic thought, during the whole of the nineteenth century had been in opposition to the abstract generalities of English classicism. American facts had suggested the German theory before it was enunciated. Veblen is perhaps the best example of an American economist who was influenced by the German school. By interesting himself in the technical and legal framework of the capitalist structure, he was able to point out social contradictions involved in business enterprise.[1]

J. B. Say, it will be remembered, saw that there was an opposition between the interests of the entrepreneur and the capitalist, although he perceived an even greater lack of harmony between the entrepreneur and the laborer (whose growing misery he deplored). Here, as elsewhere, the French economists' theory is as variegated as life and as rich in future prospect. Throughout the whole of the nineteenth century, the empirical shortsightedness of the English school did not discern the theoretical necessity for separating the entrepreneur from the capitalist until their theoretical identification became entirely untenable. The English classicists were blind to what the German economists from Schmoller to Liefmann had recognized: the similarity of private enterprise and state enterprise, and the similarity between the entrepreneur and the government official. More than that, the English writers failed to see that their own theory had been forged into an argument for socialism by the disciples of Marx and Anton Menger. The war, however, led Keynes to demonstrate how monetary depreciation accentuates the conflict between the capitalist and the entrepreneur to the profit of the latter who turns over to the capitalist the same return regardless of the level of prices. Rathenau touched on this problem of the relation between the capitalist and the entrepreneur in his visionary theory, especially in his law of general mechanization. Pareto subordinated the conflict between entrepreneurs and laborers to a more fundamental conflict between entrepreneurs and capitalists; the struggle between the creative spirit and the saving spirit; between cheap credit and dear.

[1] Cf. Hoffherr, R., "Un Nouvel Aspect du Conflit Social: Les Rapports De l'entrepreneur et du capitalisme," *Revue d'économie politique,* 1925.

While these analyses of the problem are important, it was nevertheless in the United States, for the very reason that economic life there is always magnified, that going beyond Clark, Taussig, or Seligman, we find in Thorstein Veblen the most profound and penetrating analysis of the relation between the entrepreneur and the capitalist. No one (unless it be George Sorel) has shown better than Veblen, the double character of the entrepreneur; the opposition between the technician (the captain of the industry), and the financier (the captain of affairs). Technical capital has become subordinate to legal capital, and, in this process, general interest has been sacrificed to private interest.

General interest presumes the material perfecting of enterprise, while private interests of business men may, on the contrary, be promoted by an industrial sabotage as vicious as syndicalist sabotage. Veblen estimates that the waste which results from concern with profitivity rather than productivity, a concern with "business" rather than industry, with differential rather than absolute gain, with net product rather than gross product, was equal to 300 to 1200% of the social patrimony. What is true of persons is also true of nations. Politics is only a "business" whose imperialistic and neo-mercantilistic goal is also a net product. What is there left of the classical natural regime? "The play of personal interest in a milieu of free competition," wrote Pirou in resuming the individualistic thesis, "assures economic equilibrium (since it constantly adapts production to need) and social progress (since it obliges all producers to search for technical improvements and gives the greatest reward to the most capable)." But, in reality, general interest, represented by the technical entrepreneur, is sacrificed to private interest, represented by the "business man." Both static and dynamic equilibria are thereby destroyed!

From a criticism of existing economic facts, Veblen proceeds to a criticism of their scientific expression. This he found to have two sides corresponding to the engineer and the business man. On the one hand, there is the mechanical logic of technology inspired by the Industrial Revolution; on the other hand, the monetary logic of affairs inspired by the legal evolution of the joint-stock company (an evolution which corresponds with the Industrial Revolution). In the same way that the technician yields the business man, the second of the two logics has eclipsed the first. Economists, said Veblen, are obsessed with monetary prejudices and consequently forget the technical side. No economic argument has a chance of being heard unless it is converted into a "business proposition," into an inverse relation wherein the gain of one is the loss of another. Political economy, devoted to things as they are, becomes a monographic and taxonomical science. At the same time that a desire for the static ideals yields to a preoccupation with changing reality, political economy becomes a science of "traffic," a technique. Veblen uses almost the same word as Carey. Lastly, the present tendency in American education is symbolic: a prodigious growth of "schools of business," in which the case method has been transferred from the legal to the economic sphere.[1]

But does not Veblen err in equally reproving "business economics" and "Victorian survivals"? Is not the contradiction which R. T. Bye has signalized a real one? Why criticize the detail involved in "business economics" and the generality of the old classical school from which Veblen borrowed his fundamental distinction between net and gross

[1] Cf. Veblen, Thorstein, *The Theory of Business Enterprise,* 1920; Pirou, G., *Les Doctrines Économiques en France,* 1925, p. 98; Veblen, Thorstein, "Economic Theory in the Calculable Future," *American Economic Review,* Supp. March, 1925.

product?[1] As contrasted with Veblen, W. C. Mitchell has effected a large synthesis which reconciles divergent elements. Mitchell's synthesis reconciles not only Classicism and Neo-Classicism but also fuses harmoniously mathematical and psychological tendencies (Fisher and Davenport, on the one hand; the peculiarly American psychological economics of Fetter, on the other). Thus Mitchell has achieved a synthesis which intimately allies not only the English tradition and the Austrian, but also the American statistical tradition and the historical tradition in its new form, as it is represented by Sombart, the Webbs, or Veblen.

Yet such a synthesis must remain artificial until it is impregnated with French ideology. With the English, the Austrian, the German, and the truly American currents of thought should be combined a return to the French current. Is not Veblen's revolt against modern American thought so extreme because he fails to consider the French tradition in American thought, as well as that large body of distinctly American theory of which the United States today is wrongly ashamed?

Much can be expected from a country which, in the course of the nineteenth century, could produce theorists like Raymond, Carey, and George. The youthful boastfulness of America must be overlooked. The very ability of American thinkers to pass from one philosophy to another is a promise for the future. Siegfried is an observer all too cautious to have overlooked the profoundly Rousseauistic conception of American liberty.[2] The goal of individual liberty may be reached by two paths; in one, individualism is the means, in the other, the goal. Both converge to produce individual liberty. The first relies upon free individual

---

[1] Cf. Frank, L. K., "The Emancipation of Economics," *American Economic Review*, 1924.
[2] Siegfried, A., *America Comes of Age.*

action and *laissez-faire;* it is Jeffersonian. The other looks upon individualism as a goal and urges social action to attain this goal. If the United States seems to be farther removed than Europe from the political democracy which had its origin in the "contrat social," may it not be because that nation is nearer to the convergence of these two paths, nearer to economic democracy and social exchange? The cycle of American thought is in reality a spiral in which the Hamiltonian movement cannot escape from the shadow of Jefferson.

INDEX